Patio and Pavilion

Patio and Pavilion
The Place of Sculpture in Modern Architecture

Penelope Curtis

Ridinghouse, London
The J. Paul Getty Museum, Los Angeles

INTRODUCTION

Sculpture is largely omitted from discussions of modernist architecture, but here I focus on its presence, looking at the relationship between sculpture and architecture in the mid-twentieth century. What does sculpture do to architecture, and what, in turn, does architecture do to sculpture?

The book begins with Mies van der Rohe's Barcelona Pavilion of 1929, a building that was also the starting point for my enquiry. Why does an architect add sculpture to a building that already seems perfect in itself? Asking why Mies chose Georg Kolbe's sculpture *Morning*, which is often assumed to have ended up there by mistake, led me to conclude that the choice was deliberate, for reasons that will be demonstrated.

The first half of the book takes three case-studies, separate in place and time. In each, an architect chooses to add sculpture to his architecture. In each, the sculpture adds something that the architecture alone could not provide and which the architect clearly wanted. The missing element is neither simply figurative, nor simply representative, and it may be both. The sculpture may summarise, condense or highlight the architectural experience, but it is also different from the architectural experience. These architects used sculpture—free-standing, independent sculpture—for its difference from their architecture.

The central chapter highlights a project that was never built (or even intended to be built), but which can be demonstrated to have far-reaching implications for our understanding of the relationship between sculpture and architecture in the second half of the century. Mies' museum for a hypothetical small city, one of many projects submitted to the magazine *Architectural Forum* for publication in 1943, crystallised a way of looking at sculpture in relationship to architecture which has deep connections with the construction of the space for art. Despite its conceptual nature, this project was rooted in its war-time context, and represents a developing understanding of the museum as the new monument. I will argue that its look was closely associated with a particular repertoire of sculpture, and that this duality—the open space and the fixed sculpture—was ideally suited not so much to the museum as to its extension into exterior space.

The second half of the book turns the initial question round, asking what architecture adds to sculpture. It takes another three case-studies, in each of which the sculpture collection may be taken as a given, and looks at the relationship between a designed architectural space and the sculpture it contains. The post-war sculpture garden at the Museum of Modern Art in New York took the Miesian 'court house' outside the house, as it were, and the projects of Carlo Scarpa, Gerrit Rietveld and Aldo van Eyck all use sculpture to develop the relationship between interior and exterior space. In this respect, they return very directly to the Barcelona Pavilion of Mies van der Rohe, and to the longer tradition of the pavilion as a type[1]

The architects' interest in the pavilion—or outdoor room—is consolidated by the addition of sculpture. It was the pavilion model that led to the typical modern art museum of the post-war period. The pavilion gives us transparency, but also protection. It is a special place for art—demarcated by its pedestal and

[1] The word 'pavilion' comes from the French *pavillon* and from the Latin *papilionem*. Its medieval context —which is military—links the pavilion, a two-part structure comprising curtains and roof, to the protection of the sovereign's standard. The notion of a temporary awning allowed the word to be used for other kinds of canopies or banners, on dry land and at sea, and continued to indicate allegiance. By the late seventeenth century, 'pavilion' is being used in the sense of a kiosk or amusement house. The eighteenth-century garden pavilion is transferred, by the late nineteenth century, to the pavilion from which one watches or prepares for sport. Another usage acquires currency from this time, with the advent of the Universal and Biennial Exhibition, where national representations are housed in individual temporary pavilions. An additional sense is that of the pavilion as a terminating section or extremity of a building with greater height or distinction than its neighbours.

0.1   Gerrit Rietveld, Sculpture Pavilion, model, 1954

by its canopy—which, though it may be 'in' nature, is set apart from nature. The pavilion places us on the threshold of interior and exterior. Nature and architecture are separated but joined in the person of the sculpture.

Modernist architects found a particular use for sculpture that, in part, was premised on a traditional belief in the complementary nature (but essential difference) of the two arts. The abstract and transparent qualities of modernist architecture even gave sculpture a heightened role. When sculpture diverged from its figurative form, and when architecture acquired more bodily presence, the two disciplines had less use for each other. As sculpture loses the certainty of the figurative or semi-figurative monolith, its relationship with architecture becomes less secure. When the two disciplines converge—as sculpture becomes less different from architecture, or vice-versa—their combination makes less sense. Sculptors can make their own pavilions, or architects their own sculpture. As sculpture adopts the means of the architect, the only figure to be added to the space is our own. The pavilion is still a place in which we observe nature, but it has also become a place in which we observe ourselves. There are occasions, of course, in the post-war period, when architecture does some extraordinary things for sculpture, but the special bond is broken. The essential ability of sculpture and architecture to complement one another is demonstrated rather in their collapse into one another. This book, then, looks at a specific, and rather short-lived, period.

It sets out to demonstrate that the choice to add sculpture to modernist architecture was always a deliberate one, but that it was about separation. Sculpture creates views in which the viewer is implicated, on the patio or in the pavilion, between the interior and the exterior. Thus, in addition to the mini-narratives that can be found in each chapter (what sculpture does to individual architectural spaces), the book suggests a meta-narrative, which conjoins sculpture and garden in the space of the pavilion, and looks at its scenographic constitution, with its different viewing points and distances. The whole might be identified as a historical moment that begins, and ends, with the Barcelona Pavilion. This is the thread which binds the book.

MIES' CHOICE: GEORG KOLBE IN THE BARCELONA PAVILION (1929)

[1] The Barcelona *Exposicion Internacional* was inaugurated by King Alfonso XIII in May 1929 and ran until December. The Germans had agreed to participate only in May 1928 and Mies was almost immediately given the commission. His brief changed when the authorities decided to construct an additional and independent national pavilion separate from the various trade halls. Thus Mies only began work on the pavilion as we know it in the autumn of 1928, and succeeded in shifting its allotted site to the heart of the central area, with the high blind wall of the Palau de Victoria Eugenia and the dense foliage of the gardens of Montjuic as backdrop. The building was dismantled in 1930. Fifty years later it was reconstructed, and was completed in 1986.

[2] See for example K. Frampton, 'Mies van der Rohe. Avant-garde and continuity', *Studies in Tectonic Culture*, Cambridge, Mass, 1995, p.202 or A. Drexler, *The Mies van der Rohe Archive*, New York, 1986, p.219, or J.L. Cohen, *Mies van der Rohe*, London, 1996. More recently, in his seemingly exhaustive study of the photographic representation of the Pavilion, George Dodds mentions 'three Wilhelm Lehmbruck sculptures in the preliminary plans'. *Building Desire*, London and New York, 2005, pp. 109, 119.

[3] There is no known extant correspondence between Lehmbruck and Mies and accounts of the friendship are based on family recollections.

[4] It is known from a magazine article of 1931, 'Haus Lange in Krefeld', by Walter Cohen, in *Museum der Gegenwart*, 1, no. 4, pp.160–1. The same issue includes an article on Kolbe's recent Rathenau fountain.

[5] Reich was responsible for eight of the nine exhibition areas in Gewerbehalle-platz at the centre of Stuttgart, two of which—the plate glass and linoleum displays —she designed with Mies. The Glass Room was commissioned by the Association of German Plate Glass Manufacturers; on show from 23 July to 9 October.

Mies van der Rohe's Barcelona Pavilion of 1929 has become perhaps *the* defining building of modern architecture (1.1)[1]. The sculpture inside it is neither famous nor even well-known. Georg Kolbe's *Morning* is little discussed and often mis-named. When it is mentioned, it is generally to suggest that it is a sculpture which ended up in Barcelona by mistake. Commentators, referring to Mies' friendship with the sculptor Wilhelm Lehmbruck, have often assumed that he really wanted a work by Lehmbruck for this site[2]. There is no real evidence for this supposition, and it is an assertion which blinds us to all the interesting things about the Kolbe. Moreover, the use of the Kolbe in the Barcelona Pavilion is not unique, for his work was used again by Mies in the 1931 German Building Exhibition. If we suppose that Mies wanted Kolbe's work—and we have no real reason not to— we should then ask why.

Mies van der Rohe (1886–1969) was no stranger to sculpture. His brother was a sculptor, and he was friends not only with Lehmbruck, during World War I, just before the sculptor's early death, but also with Rudolf Belling and Paul Henning[3]. Drawings for and of sculpture occur regularly in his sketchbooks, not least because he designed houses for people with modern sculpture in their personal possession. Lehmbruck's sculpture, for example, appears in photographs of the hallway and the ladies' room of the house in Krefeld (1927–30) that Mies designed for the silk industrialist Hermann Lange[4]. Thus there is a fertile crossover (which can be confusing) between real and conceptual sculptures: between those sculptures that came with the job, as it were, and those that were part of the design conception. However, a study of Mies' sketches makes it clear that sculpture peopled his vision, and that he has in mind specific pieces when he draws them. This in itself would suggest that the Kolbe could not have arrived in Barcelona *faute de mieux*. It would also suggest that Mies is not using sculpture in a generically decorative or functional way—for example, as an indicator of scale—but in a much more specific manner.

The first piece of modern sculpture to be used by Mies in his realised work would seem to be Lehmbruck's *Woman Looking Back* (*Maedchen, sich umwendend*, 1913–4). This torso first appears in the Spiegelglashalle or Glass Room[5] which he and Lilly

Mies' Choice

[6] MoMA.2.191. According to Grete Tugendhat, in a talk of 1969, the sculpture was the first 'furniture' to be delivered in the form of a drawing by Mies to his clients. See the comprehensive history of the house compiled by D. Hammer-Tugendhat and W. Tegethoff in 2000, p.7.

[7] Candian Centre for Architecture, DR 1990:0012 and 0013.

[8] According to the 1947 recollection of the young soldier Louis Schoberth (who was stationed in Brno during the war), the sculpture was cast in stone. It was lost to the Tugendhat family but re-surfaced in the stores of the Moravian Gallery in Brno and was sold at auction in 2007. See note 6 above, p.91. The torso now on show in the restored Tugendhat House is a different (dark) version.

1.1   Ludwig Mies van der Rohe, German National Pavilion, Barcelona International Exhibition, 1928–29 (demolished in 1930)

1.2   Ludwig Mies van der Rohe, The Tugendhat House, Brno, Czech Republic, 1930. View towards the conservatory showing Wilhelm Lembruck's *Torso, Girl Turning Round*, 1914

1.3   Ludwig Mies van der Rohe, The Tugendhat House, Brno, Czech Republic, 1930

Reich executed for the 1927 Stuttgart Werkbund Exhibition, *Die Wohnung*, where it occupied a significant but ambiguous position in an enclosed 'foyer', facing the dining area but looking back on a vestibule. It was thus in and out of the space of the 'house', part of and yet outside the real space of the stand. Such presentations in the vast halls of trade fairs, in which limiting walls were physically impossible and commercially undesirable, undoubtedly contributed to the various devices that Mies, and Reich, had to use in order to 'contain' their almost imaginary spaces. Seating, barriers, different floor colours and textures, pot plants in conservatories, glass screens and drapes all play their part. As does sculpture. Sculpture is human but not human. It refers us to ourselves and to a world beyond ourselves. This particular piece also moves us forward and takes us back. Like the plants, it is real but occupies a semi-illusory space on the margins of the set.

Lehmbruck's torso features again in the Tugendhat House, Brno (1928–30), appearing in a drawing for the interior,[6] as well as in some early photographs and a postcard, which show that it was an actual component of the living space, rather than playing a merely conceptual part.[7] In photographs from the Tugendhat family collection, we see the torso on a plinth, at the north-east corner of the sitting-room, marking the meeting of the glass windows, the curtain and the onyx wall. It is set on a high plinth just behind the chairs and against the screen of semi-tropical foliage in the conservatory strip beyond the windows.[8] It occupies the space between the living room and 'nature' (1.2).

Is it chance that the same torso was available to Mies so frequently in these years, or is it willed? In the Tugendhat House, the sculpture is used rather as it was in the Glass Room, and with some of the same constituents—plants, chairs, curtains, screen—with which it acts as a pivot. A closer consideration of the position of the sculpture in the Tugendhat House (1.3) takes us directly to the Barcelona Pavilion, with which it is contemporaneous. The onyx wall to the left, the chairs ranged to the right on a large rug, and the view onto a semi-enclosed world outside are remarkably similar. The difference is that the sculpture—now a Kolbe, and not a Lehmbruck, now a full-length figure and not a torso on a plinth—is taken into the outside space (1.4).

From the outset, Mies wanted sculpture in his design for the German Pavilion at the Barcelona Exhibition of 1929 (now known as the Barcelona Pavilion). Indeed, in the earliest plan for the pavilion he envisaged having three: one in each pool, and one in the central room.[9] In the event, the larger, exterior pool was left as an expanse of water unadorned by anything other than the breeze. We have no evidence as to what sculpture he was initially thinking of for the two other sites, but an interior perspective view shows a reclining figure in the interior pool.[10] As Lehmbruck made no reclining female figures, it is conceivable that Mies had in mind a work by Aristide Maillol, if indeed it is an identifiable sculpture at all. If it is, it may refer back to a reclining sculpture by Karl Albiker, which had occupied the terrace of Peter Behrens' studio when Mies had worked there before World War I.[11]

A study of Mies' use of sculpture demonstrates that it was long-lasting and remarkably consistent. This suggests that he knew—and cared about—what he was doing with sculpture. We might begin to assess

[9] CCA DR 1994:0014:004:001.

[10] A. Drexler. MVDR Archive No.14:1. Drexler assumes, however, that this drawing is in another hand.

[11] Arie Hartog referred me to this possibility, and it is now published in Ursel Berger's 'Ludwig Mies van der Rohe and Sculpture', *Barcelona Pavillon: Mies van der Rohe & Kolbe—Architecture & Sculpture*, Berlin, 2006, pp.95–6. She suggests that Behrens must have brought the figure back from the 1907 Kunst-und-Gartenbau-Ausstellung in Mannheim. Mies was working for Behrens from 1908 to 1911.

[12] At the very same time that his work was being used by Mies, Kolbe was designing his own new studio in Berlin, against which he positioned his most recent sculptures. Thus a building of 1928 was accompanied by sculptures of the same period. In the 1914 Werkbund Exhibition, Kolbe's *Large Bather* had been positioned in front of contemporaneous buildings by Gropius and Van de Velde.

[13] The Exhibition was of the Münchener Künstler-Genossenschaft; the six rooms were each designed by different architects. Kolbe's *Grosse Statue* in plaster (No. 466a) was shown in room 6, the *Kolbe-Saal*, designed by Wilhelm Kreis, with his other works mounted on brick pedestals around about it. The ensemble, a collaboration between Kreis and Kolbe, was carefully worked out in terms of the cohesion of the surface treatment and of the rhythm of the sculptures. The bricks that made up the pedestals and their linking walls were bigger than the very fine bricks that lined the gallery walls, and which were arranged in two bands. The whole was lit from above, rather as if it were a Roman impluvium.

[14] The Ceciliengaerten housing scheme was initiated in 1912, delayed, and then completed between 1924 and 1926. (continues overleaf)

1.4   Ludwig Mies van der Rohe, Barcelona Pavilion, reconstructed in 1986, Barcelona. Georg Kolbe's *Morning,* 1925 in water court

what sculpture did for his architecture with Kolbe's *Morning.* Unlike the works of Lehmbruck and Maillol, Kolbe's sculptures are contemporaneous with Mies' practice.[12] But while *Morning* is, prima facie, contemporary, in that it dates to 1925, do we necessarily accept that Kolbe was as modern—in his way—as Mies? Is this what modern sculpture looks like, even if it looks more old-fashioned than the architecture? Or is this what a modern architect wanted from sculpture, even if it was not the most modern?

Morning had been shown at the Munich Glaspalast exhibition in 1927 and if Mies did not see it here, where it was a centrepiece of the show,[13] he may already have seen it in Berlin's Ceciliengarten, where it was placed alongside its pendant, *Evening* (with which it is often confused). Neither title is in fact constant, and the Ceciliengarten sculptures were originally known simply as just that.[14] Their unveiling was published in *Kunst und Kuenstler* of March 1926, and the illustrations show the works on their original cubic travertine plinths.[15] It is also quite possible that Mies visited Kolbe's studio in Berlin to choose a sculpture

that suited his purpose. He had little time in the execution of the Barcelona Pavilion, and to choose from existing sculptures was the most effective way of arriving at the solution that he must already have come close to understanding.[16] He knew he needed a sculpture which would work outdoors, in other words that was not a partial figure on a plinth, and which spoke in the right way. Mies chose *Morning*, and not *Evening*, and it can be demonstrated why he might have made this choice.[17]

Both *Morning* and *Evening* have a ponderous slowness about them. They seem to push at the air as if it had density and weight. They look down, away from the viewer, while engaged in a trance-like and almost circular play around their own bodies. While *Evening* (1.5)—whose arms are lowered and held stiffly away from the body—looks down diagonally

[14] Discussion of the scheme, and of Kolbe's sculptures, was sufficiently widespread at the time for it to have been possible for Mies to have noticed them in this way. During the partition of Germany, the sculptures were treated as separate pieces and placed in three different sites in Berlin-Schoeneberg but in 1990 they were reinstated in the garden on new (and lower) plinths. In a 1931 catalogue of Kolbe photographs available from the Marburg Archive, the statues are entitled 'Caecilienstatue I and II', both 2.45m and dated to 1925.

[15] 'Zwei Statuen von Georg Kolbe', *Kunst und Kuenstler*, 20 March 1926, p.297.

[16] Wolf Tegethoff, in the most succinct account of the pavilion, quotes a telegram from Mies to Reich of February 22, 1929 (MoMA): 'Give Kaiser the photo of

the Kolbe sculpture and the book on Lehmbruck so that [we can] negotiate with the appropriate gentleman here.' *Mies van der Rohe: The Villas and Country Houses* (English edition), New York, 1985, p.81

[17] It was the tinted plaster as shown in Munich that went to Barcelona.

1.5   Georg Kolbe, *Evening,* 1925, Ceciliengarten, Berlin

1.6   Georg Kolbe, *Morning,* 1925, Ceciliengarten, Berlin

1.7   Georg Kolbe, *Morning,* 1925

and seems to push the air behind her, *Morning's* movement is more syncopated, and the slow unfurling of the arms above the head, with the marked bending of both knees, is distinctly more beguiling (1.6). This is especially true if the sculptures are compared from the front. From the back, however, the joined legs of *Morning* constitute a rather ugly monolith (1.7), whereas *Evening*, with her legs apart and slightly contraposto, reads more sympathetically. *Morning* is much more successful if it can only be viewed from the front, and if the figure's downwards glance makes sense in combination with what is in the surrounding space. In Barcelona, Mies provided her with a most sympathetic setting (1.8).

'Morning' and 'Evening' are commonplace titles—or subjects—for sculptures, and one might argue that there is nothing meaningful in Mies choosing *Morning*

Mies' Choice

[18] A chronology of the statue's travels is given on page 25 of *Der Betende Knabe, Original und Experiment* by Gerhard Zimmer and Nele Hacklaender, Frankfurt am Main, 1997. It was on the terrace at Sanssouci from 1747 to 1786.

[19] At the Casino in Schloss Glienicke, Berlin, 1824–5.

1.8   Georg Kolbe, 'Morning' 1925. Ludwig Mies van der Rohe, Barcelona Pavilion, reconstructed in 1986, Barcelona

in particular. Nevertheless, it is also possible to suggest that there is something more at play. In Berlin, in his design for the Urbig House of 1915–16, Mies had used a copy of the antique sculpture *Der Betende Knabe* (The Praying Boy). This figure had an almost central role in the consciousness of sculpture's relationship to architecture, and above all in Berlin. In the eighteenth century Frederick the Great had placed it, facing away from the window, as part of the view from his library at the Sanssouci palace in Potsdam (1.9). In 1830, it was transferred from outdoors to indoors with Karl Friedrich Schinkel's creation of the Altes Museum, where it once again occupies a central position.[18] It had gone from being in the view to being the viewer. Thus this is a sculpture which held a key position in the visual memory of Berlin, and which Mies had already used in reproduction (as had many architects, including Schinkel himself).[19] Moreover, *The Praying Boy* was thought to represent a prayer, or greeting, to the morning sun (1.10). Is it not possible that Mies had this image in his mind when he chose *Morning* as the work which was at one and the same time the view and the viewer, on the outside and in the inside of his ceremonial pavilion? *Morning* greets the sun, and it greeted the royal guests who preceded the many other visitors to this pretend piece of real estate.

Should we see Kolbe's work as in the tradition of classical sculpture—and therefore its placing in the Barcelona pavilion as in the tradition of Schinkel's use of *The Praying Boy*? Or can we see it as equally modern—if differently modern—as the pavilion itself? How do we understand the relation between 'old-fashioned' sculpture and new-fashioned spaces? We are left with two possibilities. One is that Mies chose such sculpture in clear contrast to what he was doing as an architect. The other is that he deliberately chose it as echoing or paraphrasing his architecture. The sculpture is like a reprise of the visitor's dream-like passage around the travertine pedestal, with its variously transparent or reflective panels of water, glass and coloured marble.

If we can understand this sculpture as modern, then we can also understand why it might be the right corollary for an architecture that offers transitional and over-lapping zones in a manner open to its viewer's experience. *Morning* (1.11) is centrifugal (whereas

Evening is centripetal); it opens outwards, rippling, in a manner suggestive of the pool where it stands, and the building around it. Some of the older black and white photographs documenting the Barcelona Pavilion cast *Morning* in the more or less traditional role of eye-catcher, providing a focal point for the viewer, leading the eye and telling it where to rest. It throws its viewers back on the manner in which they have just experienced the space where it stands. It absorbs and reiterates, phrasing an extended physical experience in more narrowly figurative terms, representing in a single narrative the longer journey around the 'garden' in which it is placed. In a house of mirrors, the statue might be seen to provide a point of engagement, even if that engagement is shifting.[20] But photographs (old and new) can also prove how the sculpture can itself participate in this game of illusion, its green patina merging with the green of the Alpine marble and the foliage above. Its body—and

[20] CCA DR 1994:0014:004:008.

[21] CCA DR 1994:0014:006:002.

1.9   Copy of the antique sculpture *Der Betende Knabe* (The Praying Boy), on the terrace at Sanssouci Palace, Potsdam

1.10   *Der Betende Knabe* (The Praying Boy), bronze, Antikensammlung, Staatliche Museen zu Berlin

the message of its body—are similarly ambiguous.

In the 1931 German Building Exhibition in Berlin, Mies would again place a sculpture by Kolbe in an exterior courtyard beside a pool. A documentary photograph of that installation suggests something of the photographic negative, in that the plaster is untinted and thus strikingly white.[21] This gives the whole image an aspect of the inside-out, or to go further, provides the building with its own ghost. The use of plaster was nothing new in itself; it was merely a continuation of the nineteenth-century tradition of using this material for temporary structures and, perhaps more importantly, for effect. But the photograph goes further, in showing how, placed against the transparent modernism of Mies' House for a Childless Couple, the plaster sculpture had a remarkable effect. And the photograph also reveals how very effectively sculptural profile could carry in two dimensions.

Mies' Choice

[22] See Detlef Mertins' 'Architectures of Becoming' in *Mies in Berlin*, New York, 2001, p.128.

[23] Details from Grete Tugendhat (at note 6) and from Raymond McGrath, *Glass in Architecture and Decoration*, London, 1937, p.370 (1961 edition, p.200).

[24] See D. Hammer-Tugendhat/Wolf Tegethoff (eds), *Ludwig Mies van der Rohe, The Tugendhat House*, Vienna, 2000, p.181 for modern colour photographs of the restoration.

[25] The review in *Cahiers d'Art* (8–9, 1929, p.409) acknowledges this at the outset: 'C'est de l'architecture représentative, comme un obélisque ou un arc de triomphe.'

[26] The best account is given in J.P. Bonta, *An Anatomy of Architectural Interpretation*, Barcelona, 1975.

1.11   Georg Kolbe, *Morning*, 1925, in the water court of Ludwig Mies van der Rohe's Barcelona Pavilion, reconstructed in 1986, Barcelona

If black and white photography shows plaster sculptures to admirable effect, colour photography reveals other similarities between Mies' spaces. The spaces in the Tugendhat House and in the Barcelona Pavilion take on another aspect in the new colour photos of the restored or reconstructed buildings, an aspect which they must have shared with the Glass Room, although it is pictured only in black and white. We know from textual descriptions that the Glass Room was richly coloured and comprised four shades of glass, including grey and olive green and a linoleum floor in white, grey and red.[22] In the Tugendhat House, also furnished by Lilly Reich, the pale sculpture was set against the golden onyx wall, beside velvet and silk curtains in black and silver. It was offset by furniture in a silver-grey Rodier material, emerald green leather and red velvet, on a rug of 'undyed wool on a floor of white linoleum'[23] (Modern photographs show chairs with black, white and red upholstery.)[24] The central space of the Barcelona Pavilion also used colours to good effect: the golden onyx wall, black carpet and red curtains reprise the German flag. This building was, after all, designed as a *repraesentationspavilion*, even if its symbolic centre was to cede some importance to its exterior spaces.[25] Colour helps us, above all, to understand more clearly how the interior was constituted in distinction to the exterior.

Against these richly coloured interiors lie the greens of the garden. In Brno, tropical conservatory plants were the first backdrop, bordering the windows and the little indoor pool, beyond which lay the second backdrop of the Central European garden. In Barcelona, the green Alpine marble was the still German 'garden', against which the trees of the foreign city trembled. It represented the garden beyond the ceremonial space where the Spanish King and Queen would be welcomed onto 'German soil'. Some of the earliest commentaries on the pavilion—which was by no means widely appreciated or even noted at the time[26]—define it within the tradition of garden architecture, and come from English writers of the 1930s. Both Raymond McGrath and Christopher Tunnard called the pavilion a 'garden house' almost as if this were its title. Neither McGrath in his 1934 book *Twentieth-Century Houses*, nor Tunnard in his 1938 book on *Gardens in the Modern Landscape*, mention any of the pavilion's specific and symbolic purposes, simply captioning it as a 'garden house'

Mies' Choice

tout court. In his next book, McGrath described what he calls the 'water-garden'—the 'black glass wall of the terrace [which] darkly gives back the moving leaves of the garden'[27]—and Tunnard echoes McGrath: 'The black glass walls reflect with curious depth the pattern of the surrounding water garden'[28] McGrath's caption further refers to Claude Lorraine glasses and to Christopher Hussey's book on the picturesque, thus inserting the pavilion into an English tradition of eighteenth-century landscape architecture[29] Can we see *Morning* as belonging to the tradition of garden sculpture, isolated as the statue is in its pool, pulling the eye towards it from afar?

But is *Morning* outside the Barcelona pavilion or inside it? While in a sense the pavilion excludes the exterior, in another sense it captures and contains it (1.12). Focusing on *Morning* helps us to understand how Mies is using nature. As he brings nature inside the house, by the use of transparency, so he needs to bring inside the sculpture, which would traditionally have been outdoors[30] His early formation as an architect with Peter Behrens, its deep association with 'space-forming' by means of garden landscaping, going back in particular to the work of Schinkel, is exquisitely realised in this corner of an exhibition ground in Barcelona. The use of sculpture asserts nature's capture, their mergent qualities at once an artifice and a reality. The pavilion is a belvedere, but instead of looking out at the view from its platform, the view is inside, and we circle around it.

Mies knew what he wanted from sculpture and he remained remarkably faithful to this vision. The sculptures which he chose in the late 1920s and during the 1930s were to serve him to the end of his career, and the kinds of relationships which he created in Barcelona established the space for art that appears in his work (and that of others) from then on. The pool —sheltered and still, almost uncannily dark—acts as another reflective surface in a space of mirrors[31] Its protective outer wall is as two-dimensional as a wall can be, and even the trees above are reduced to something close to a photographic collage[32] The textures of water and leaves are like the endless (rippling) screens that will appear in Mies' work within the next decade: the 'garden' in Barcelona is echoed by the later collages for a museum, which place defined artworks against an indistinct flat screen of

[27] R. McGrath, *Twentieth-Century Houses,* London, 1934, p.168. It is conceivable that by the later 1930s this was a deliberate ploy to distance the pavilion from its official national origins.

[28] In chapter IV, 'Art and Ornament', *Gardens in the Modern Landscape,* London, 1938, p.105.

[29] McGrath, 1961/37, op. cit., p.382.

[30] CCA DR 1994:0014:004:010.

[31] It was lined with black glass tiles.

[32] CCA DR 1994:0014:004:009.

1.12   (previous pages) Georg Kolbe, *Morning,* 1925. Ludwig Mies van der Rohe, Barcelona Pavilion, reconstructed in 1986, Barcelona. View towards water court from interior

foliage or water. The roving, browsing eye is stilled by sculpture, or rather asked to operate in a different way. Sculpture is given life by nature, and mass is given a backdrop. Nature is flattened, but moves, like a film, without edges. This is scenography, and the sculpture is the player. Sculpture does more than elide inside and out—in itself a classical trope—but heightens the meaning of both.

Mies wanted Kolbe's *Morning* for a specific purpose, and it developed the work he had already accomplished in combining sculpture and architecture. If its distant cousin was *The Praying Boy*, its contemporary was Lehmbruck's 'torso', positioned in front of the conservatory of the Tugendhat House. But it went further than either in acting, on the one hand, as an axial eye-catcher or fixed point, and on the other, as a hidden, or moving target, which continually reappears in this transparent, reflective building. It beckons, but is ultimately unattainable, isolated as it is within its pool. It is not just a curiosity that we must accept in the pavilion, but a component that is crucial to the architecture's meaning. The sculpture not only gives the building a human quality, but illuminates its architectural ones too. It encapsulates the journey we have just taken, and promises its endless repetition, inside or out.

PERSICO'S VISION: LUCIO FONTANA AT THE MILAN TRIENNALE (1936)

[1] In his 1938 *Arte Decorativa Italiana*, the architect Giuseppe Pagano made the case for seeing the Triennale as a way of escaping the fruitless separation of the arts and allowing different kinds of artists to work together. In his view, Mario Sironi's mosaic on the staircase and the Salone della Vittoria were the most important examples of modern monumental decoration.

[2] The first competition was for furniture, the second for a dining room with mural decoration.

[3] Paraphrased from the description for the competition given by Persico in *La Casa Bella*, February 1935, from *Edoardo Persico. Tutte le opere (1923–1935)*, ed. G. Veronesi, Milan, 1964, vol 2, p.154. The judges included the largely conservative architect Marcello Piacentini and sculptor Antonio Maraini, as well as painter Sironi and architect Pagano.

[4] Fascist competitions were supposed to be reserved for members of the syndicates or unions; Persico was not a member, but Palanti, Nizzoli and Fontana were.

[5] The translations are mine. This paragraph alone is from the reproduction of the competition entry in *Edoardo Persico*, ed. C. De Seta, Naples, 1987, p.141. All the others are taken from reproductions in G. Veronesi's collection of Persico's writings.

Since almost the outset of the Fascist regime, the Milan Triennale exhibitions had not simply showcased collaborative ventures in the applied arts, but had sought to define an Italian modernity for a national and an international audience. These exhibitions—the *International Exhibitions of Decorative Arts*—were first held in Monza, as biennales, from 1923. In 1930, they became triennial, and in 1931 were officially transferred from Monza to Milan to give them more prominence. Their full title was now *Esposizioni triennali internazionali delle arte decorative ed industriali moderne e dell'architettura moderna*. The 1933 exhibition, the V Triennale, was the first to be held in Milan. While their purpose was still to showcase the best in modern applied arts and design, during the 1930s they also became a key experimental showplace for modernism, bringing together different disciplines in over-arching exhibition concepts that remained remarkably free of the more heavy-handed classicism emanating from Rome.

The VI Milan Triennale was held from May to October 1936.[1] Three competitions for the decoration of the Palazzo dell'Arte were announced in advance,[2] the third of which was a project for the Salone d'Onore, intended 'to give artists a way of confirming their collective maturity in devoting themselves to decorative works for large spaces with a representative character'.[3] The critic and designer Edoardo Persico (1900–36) entered this competition with his chosen collaborators, the architect Giancarlo Palanti and artist Marcello Nizzoli.[4] The text of their winning submission ran as follows:

> I   The scope of the project is to create not a simple decoration of the existing room, but within its spatial limits to create a new architecture following an independent and original rhythm.

> II   According to a classical principal, which modern architecture has taken to its fullest extreme, the architectonic composition of the walls corresponds to the concept of a continuous rhythm: the most suited to works of monumental character.[5]

> III   Take the existing room as merely a spatial limit. The structure of the new room also abolishes the system of doors and substitutes

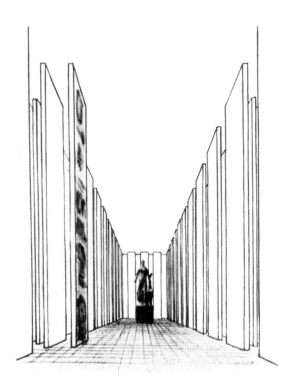

for it a plurality of entrances, adhering to the nature of the architectonic composition.

IV   In the project the sculpture and the tessallated works are not thought of as 'decoration', or as parts added to the architecture, but more or less constitute the argument by means of their stereometry and by the intimate stylistic adherence.

V   The particular disposition of the vertical panels [diaframmi] plays a game of light and dark and a rapport between full and empty, leading almost to the expression of a pure logic. Thus the antique aspect of the colonnades assumes, in the project, a real figurative value.

VI   In the wall in front of the sculpture the throne can be located. For the style of the throne we imagine maintaining that consecrated by heraldic tradition as being the most representative of regal authority (2.1).

[6] This interpretation is found in Giulia Veronesi's note to the original text for the three competitions ('Tre Concorsi'), which had been published in *La Casa Bella* in February 1935. Though it might have been in Veronesi's interest, in 1964, to insist on the less imperialistic nature of the original project, it is also clear that the project was announced well before the Italian 'victory' in Ethiopia/Abyssinia. See Veronesi, p.154.

2.1   Edoardo Persico, Marcello Nizzoli, Giancarlo Palanti. Salone d'Onore at the VI Milan Triennale, 1936 (Competition Drawings)

This Salone d'Onore—or Room of Honour—became known as the Sala della Vittoria—or Room of Victory. It also became known, through contemporary criticism and photography, as an extraordinary space. It has consistently impressed those who study it, whether or not they like what it stands for. To what extent Persico can be seen as the author of a pacifist vision, which took the triumphalism out of Fascist display, is debatable. Persico had died prematurely five months before the Triennale opened, and even if the plan was therefore changed in its realisation, the concept is impressive in the way that Fascist exhibitions were impressive: awe-inspiring spectacles designed to stir the emotions instinctively rather than intellectually.

The room was executed by Palanti and Nizzoli; the sculpture was by Lucio Fontana. Some details were indeed modified after Persico's death and as circumstances changed following the Italian campaign in Africa.[6] Though the throne was abolished, the room in fact acquired a more triumphalist title, and text, after Mussolini's declaration of Empire shortly before the Triennale opened. What had been a 'room of honour' now became a 'room of victory', and the text on the socle of the sculpture (2.2) ran as follows:

IL POPOLO ITALIANO HA
CREATO COL SUO SANGUE
L'IMPERO. LO FECONDERA
COL SUO LAVORO E LO DIFEN
DERA CONTRO CHIUNQUE
CON LE ARMI. MUSSOLINI 9 V XIV[7]

Though the text might shift the room's signification, the key components of the competition project—the temple-like colonnade, the sculpture and the portraits of five Roman Emperors[8] (or *condottieri*)—remained constant. Moreover, they all have intimate links with the work that Persico had developed in the recent past, or with the work that he admired.[9]

Over the course of 1934, Nizzoli and Persico had collaborated on other structures which combined an architectonic framework with a representative message.[10] In two projects in Milan—the temporary scaffoldings erected in the Galleria Vittorio Emanuele and the Sala delle Medaglie d'Oro at the Italian Aeronautical Exhibition—the 'content' was displayed in the form of photographs and texts applied to an open grid-like linear framework. In both, the content was 'dense' while the architecture was light and open. In the Galleria, the new structure was shown against the dense fabric of the old arcade, the barrel vaults of which actually echo the linear framework of the scaffolding. In the Aeronautical Exhibition, the floor and ceiling were black and the central panel white, against which the black and white photography and texts stood out.

Persico was the editor, with Giuseppe Pagano, of the magazine *Casabella,* and his work as a graphic designer (and teacher) undoubtedly fed into his work as a scenographer. His layouts for this magazine speak clearly of his interest in black and white imagery, in texture, rhythm and in the use of discrete colour. His 1935 photo essay *Arte Romana* (a supplement to *Domus*)[11] again reveals his careful typographic design, but speaks above all of the enigmatic and engaging stillness of sculpture, with its large, arresting images of Roman portrait heads. The collection might sound

[7] 'The Italian people have created the Empire with their blood. They will make it fertile with their work and will defend it against whomsoever with their arms.' From a broadcast speech by Mussolini, 9 May 1936 (Year XIV of the regime). The Italian campaign in Ethiopia (Abyssinia) lasted from October 1935 to May 1936; on 5 May they took Addis Ababa, on 7 May they annexed Eritrea, Abyssinia and Somaliland and on 9 May they declared King Victor Emmanuel Emperor.

[8] Scipio, Caesar, Augustus, Trajan and Constantine. Reference is made by Richard Etlin, in his discussion of this project, to Giovanni Viganoni's 1933 *Mussolini e i cesari*. The photographs used by Nizzoli are not, however, close to those in this small-format book, which makes overt links between the leadership of Mussolini (who is represented by a bust by Adolf Wildt) and that of seventeen Roman emperors, from Caesar to Justinian.

[9] Persico (a Neapolitan) came to Turin in 1928 and to Milan in 1929, invited there by P.M. Bardi to run his magazine *Belvedere* and the gallery that became Il Milione. His circle included Fontana, Fausto Melotti, Carlo Belli, Gino Pollini and Luciano Baldessari. Working for architects and designers such as Figini and Pollini, Baldessari and BBPR, Fontana supplied what might be termed the figurative and representative elements of their structures, in the form of horses and people. Nizzoli and Melotti fulfilled a similar role.

[10] In addition to more purely commercial work, for the Parker Pen Company, for example.

[11] Supplement of December 1935; its full title being *Arte Romana: La scultura romana e quattro affreschi della villa dei misteri*. Also published, in Italy in 1936, as *Sculptures Romaines: De César à Justinien*.

2.2   Edoardo Persico, Marcello Nizzoli, Giancarlo Palanti. Salone d'Onore at the VI Milan Triennale, 1936

traditional, but the careful adherence to similarity of type, scale and angle has the effect of a design which transcends its self-imposed rules to become a work of art.

Arte Romana is oversize in format, and uses black sugar paper as well as glossy paper. The *mise-en-page* of the eighty illustrations is by Persico, and alongside the more detailed photographs of Roman reliefs, the portrait heads stare out mute but eloquent. Over a foot high, each head is (or is close to) life size, and is presented as a cut-out on a black or a white background. Persico had found a way of presenting antique sculpture in a way that was fresh, direct and contemporary. The apparently straightforward documentary (almost journalistic) approach rose above its origins and became something else.

The Salone d'Onore took some of the elements of the Sala delle Medagalie d'Oro and simplified them. Gone was the grid framework, but the light was similarly diffused, emerging from behind long vertical panels (or diaphragms) lining the walls in a double row. It was bright, however, using large numbers of high wattage bulbs that left the viewers blinking.

Imagery was reduced and intensified: Nizzoli's five portraits of Roman Emperors were pixellated as if they were enlarged photographs (ie, as if they were propaganda images) though they were in fact made with a cement inlay (*intarsio de cimento*; a kind of double transformation of means). These 'photomosaics' are historical figures presented by means of a modern medium. Displaced, out of time, they are perhaps more modern than ancient, but vacillate between the two. Referencing an authority of the past, they nevertheless unerringly allude to the authority of the present.

The central image of the room was both dominant (enormous and central) and curiously without body (2.3). Lucio Fontana's female figure, standing on one plinth, followed by two rampant horses on a second, larger plinth directly behind, was made of white plaster. In the intense illumination of the room, the horses and the woman must have emerged like a dream, visible and invisible, hard to pin down and to see in any detail. The standard 'stuff' of exhibition statuary—that is to say white plaster—was here

[12] 'All'estremità della modernità: Mies van der Rohe', reprinted in Veronesi, pp.54–6.

[13] Fontana supplied the Victory figure for Terragni's war memorial at Erba (1926–32), a relief that was installed at the back of the sacrarium.

2.3   Edoardo Persico, Marcello Nizzoli, Giancarlo Palanti. Salone d'Onore at the VI Milan Triennale, 1936

made to work to full effect. Its whiteness seems both to evoke history—not just classical casts, but also the plaster casts of Pompeian figures—and to look forward, like the *tabula rasa* or the *carte blanche* of a new beginning. The trope is traditional but the sculptural treatment is unfamiliar. Like much of Fontana's work of the time, the form seems at once to be eroded—whittled away like a bone—and in the process of becoming. Like Nizzoli, but to an even greater extent, Fontana gave Persico what he needed, making strange familiar themes. The sculptures are large, but attenuated; solid but fragile; assertive yet questioning. They fundamentally hint at their own imminent collapse (2.4). Their clothes, as much like rags as drapery, heighten the auratic mood, lending a greater irreality and distancing the sculptures from the more conventional Beaux-Arts statuary.

Persico's concept can be interpreted as a room of honour, or throne room, in the shape of a temple. We might well compare it to the Barcelona Pavilion, another honorific space, which also had its own 'thrones', presented on a pedestal reminiscent of a temple. (And Persico was one of the few architectural critics to notice and to speak favourably of the pavilion in his short article on Mies' modernity in *La Casa Bella* in November 1931.)[12] One is open, one closed. Both are light, and both disorienting. One is dispersed, one axial, but neither reveals itself rapidly. Both refer, if obliquely, to the origins of the pavilion as the canopied resting-place of the royal standard.

In their modern temples, both Mies and Persico use modern sculpture in an apparently old-fashioned way (2.5). Mies chose an existing work; Persico to commission an artist whose work he had already noticed in exhibitions and about which he had written. Both were in plaster. Both are given 'pride of place', if in different ways. Kolbe's is clearly only one of many equal parts, while Fontana's work might read more obviously as simultaneously the subject of and the object for the container.

Whether or not it was accompanied by its text, Fontana's (wingless) Nike figure is surely victorious, and the fact that it was Fontana's Victory figures which had particularly attracted Persico's attention in his earlier texts is not without relevance for our reading of its meaning.[13] In *La Casa Bella* of August 1932,

Persico observed that the 'Victory' of Fontana, which he had earlier admired at the Galleria del Milione, now graced Terragni's War memorial at Erba. He noted that Fontana's work was perhaps 'the only practice in Italy to represent the art of new sculptors in the long series of monuments inspired by antiquated sculptural habits'. It was, he claimed, 'An affirmation of all our avant-garde art, which, with Fontana's *Victory*, logically claims the prize in civic commemoration.'[14]

In comparison to Fontana's irreality, Mies' choice of Kolbe seems to offer a kind of reality. *Morning* is c.2.5 metres high, but the Fontana pieces were around 6 metres, judging by contemporary photographs in which visitors are no higher than the plinth on which the sculpture stands.[15] Fontana's sculpture must have been hallucinatory, whereas that of Kolbe is, at most, spectral. An Italian critic, annotating his copy of Persico's writing, describes this *chiarismo* (or brightness) as a polemical style:

> They all began to make things white. And so the paintings were all white…the frames were white, left in pure plaster, and the exhibitions looked like they were in their underclothes, and the painting was white as if it had stomach ache, and at the Triennale, the grand salon, imperial-Roman, by Lucio Fontana and by Persico, was all in white. You needed sunglasses.[16]

Fascist exhibition technique is not about illumination, but about stupefaction, and if we see *Morning* as being about learning to see, then the Fontana might well be seen as its inverse. *Morning* represents the woman waking up, or shielding her eyes from the light, and in this sense is both about us (the natural human response to rising light) and about the tradition of sculpture in general.[17] *Morning* may not be the subject of the Barcelona Pavilion, but it helps us to see that building. It is a kind of marginal punctuation mark, a respite within a disorienting space, whereas Fontana's work was all about disorientation.

If the Barcelona Pavilion and its restrained statuary is understood cautiously to suggest a different sense of what Germany might mean in 1929, the Salone della Vittoria certainly suggests what Italy means in 1936.

Unusually for practitioners working under the Fascist

[14] 'Un'affermazione di tutta la nostra arte d'avanguardia che, con la Vittoria di Fontana, rivendica logicamente il primato nelle celebrazioni civili.' 'La "Vittoria" di Fontana', from *La Casa Bella,* August 1932, reprinted in Persico, op. cit., vol. 1, p. 150. He wrote on Fontana again in *L'Italia Letteraria* (4 August 1934) and in a text for a book published posthumously. Both are reproduced in the above collection, pp.188–192.

[15] And according to the artist's own calculation, as cited by Paolo Campiglio in a note, *Lucio Fontana: la scultura architettonica degli anni trenta*, Nuoro, 1995, note 140, p.145.

[16] 'tutti si mettevano a far bianco. E così vedeva i quadri tutti bianchi…e le cornici furono bianche, lasciate in gesso puro, e le mostre parvero tutte in mutande, e la pittura fu in bianco come fe…malati di stomace, e alla triennale il gran salone romano-imperiale, di Lucio Fontana, e di Persico, fu tutto in bianco. Ci volevano gli occhiali neri'. Manuscript note by reader (one presumes by Leonardo Borgese, 1904–86, art critic of *Corriere della Sera* from 1945 to 1967) in *Edoardo Persico. Scritti Critici e Polemici*, Milan, 1947, ed. A. Gatto in the Getty's Borgese collection.

[17] See above, Chapter I, and Bergdoll, 'The Nature of Mies' Space', in *Mies in Berlin*, New York, 2001, p.81.

2.4   Edoardo Persico, Marcello Nizzoli, Giancarlo Palanti. Salone d'Onore at the VI Milan Triennale, 1936

regime in Italy, Persico had a determinedly contemporary view of how to use antique sculpture.[18] In his introduction to the *Arte Romana* collection, he had explicitly stated this to be his aim. Asking how the public was to succeed in 'seeing' Roman sculpture, he answers: from the standpoint of modern taste, using the experience of modern art to understand the antique. Persico took the themes common to the regime—including the horse and rider and the figure of Victory—and had them interpreted by an artist capable of re-invigorating and of questioning forms such as those of the Dioscuri, the twin horse-tamers. Unlike other contemporary usages of the antique, Fontana's seems at once to be inspired by the monumental and propagandist energy of the Facist regime and, and in this scheme above all, to destabilise it.

It has, perhaps, been too easy for Persico's admirers to distance him from Fascism. In fact the Salone d'Onore carries many characteristics of recent Fascist architectural projects and competitions, including the shrine-like quality of the inner sanctum, the representation of sacrifice (and it is understood that the original scheme included a single 'pool' or *tache* of red, thereby indicating the blood of Fascist martyrs), and the slab or grave-like quality of the 'message'. Whether or not such markers are distanced from their usual content by the extreme modernity of this particular concept—that the sanctum was blindingly white, that the red mark would thus have been extraordinarily vivid, that the slab showed disconcertingly expanded Imperial portraits —is open to question.[19]

The Salone has qualities of tomb architecture (as did many of the early Fascist projects), and Fontana's vocabulary is never far removed from the cemetery. Marble-clad mausolea and carefully fabricated family tombs, each a miniature home or temple, make real links between funerary and fine art. Fontana's tomb commissions, mostly in the Milan Monumental Cemetery, span his career, and mirror not only his own evolution, but that of modern art more widely. They reveal his astute response to the concept of figurative resurrection in relation to the horizontal and the vertical of the ground and of the gravemarker. The 1936 *Vittoria* in Persico's scheme can be compared to Fontana's remarkable risen black and gold Christ on the 1935 Castellotti tomb. This, too, is a

[18] A comparison is in the montage, shown in *Casabella*, of the BBPR pavilion for the Paris Exposition of 1937, which uses photographs of the bas-reliefs from the Arch of Titus to stand in for the reliefs which Fontana would supply. On Fontana's monumental work of this period, see Paolo Campiglio, *La scultura architettonica negli anni Trenta*, Nuoro, 1995.

[19] There are plenty of modernist schemes that included the Fascist Sacrarium—including Terragni's outstanding Casa del Fascio—so it is difficult to distance Persico from this near-standard iconography by reason of the modernity of his concept.

2.5   Edoardo Persico, Marcello Nizzoli, Giancarlo Palanti. Salone d'Onore at the VI Milan Triennale, 1936

IL POPOLO ITALIANO HA
CREATO COL SUO SANGUE
L'IMPERO, LO FECONDERÀ
COL SUO LAVORO E LO DIFEN
DERÀ CONTRO CHIUNQUE
CON LE ARMI. MUSSOLINI

figure which seems to rise and fall, to move forward and back, to take form and to disperse.

Persico had understood something about Roman sculpture which was rarely perceived. Whereas classical forms were in these years very often repeated, enlarged, and nullified in the process, Persico made them new by doing the same thing. Repetition and reproduction is integral to the interest of this language. Nizzoli manifests this seriality, in old and in new form, and Fontana its enlargement. In the Sala della Vittoria, Pagano considered Persico to have achieved a perfect accord between architecture and figurative art, and a synthesis in the two key elements of modern architecture: the practical question of serial construction and the aesthetic question of expression.[20]

In 1935, Persico lauded Fontana's most recent works, protecting the sculptor from accusations of being bizarre or paradoxical and stressing instead his 'extreme coherence'. In Persico's view they showed his critical astuteness, and his force in submitting European taste to his own rationalism.

> In these works, every external stylistic preoccupation has been laid aside, and the artist is thus ready to resolve a classical motif with the felicity of a Lehmbruck or of a de Fiori ... This is the 'impressionism' of Fontana: the capacity for lively and immediate expression.[21]

Fontana is rarely compared to Lehmbruck, and rarely described as 'expressive'. He has been primarily lauded for his post-war (post-Fascist) career, in which he is known for his formal (abstract) innovations. But his figurative style is under-discussed, despite (or because of) its mysterious quality.

Almost all Fontana's figures from the 1930s have an ambiguity that is hard to define. They are at once strong and weak, and it is hard to know if this is a strength or a weakness, and whether it is knowing or unconscious. They point to the death of figurative art (and to the virtues it is used to represent) while employing the figure to do so. It undermines itself. And this is not unlike Lehmbruck, whose attentuated forms seem to disappear into themselves, as if they have no will to go on. But whereas Lehmbruck's forms have clean, strong profiles, Fontana's are generally

ragged, and his expression lies largely on the modelled surface. The 1934 *Vittoria dell'aria*, made for the Aeronautical exhibition, for example, is the most curious of Victory figures. A dishevelled woman, edging forward as if to impart some kind of news, seems to be on the edge of losing control (2.6).[22]

Fontana's indeterminacy seems to suit Persico's Salone d'Onore remarkably well, not only merging with its radiance, but enhancing its message as a container of a revivified classical language. It is monumental but not monumental, classical and modern. It does not so much answer doubts about Persico's success in reclaiming the classical tradition from the regime, as raise them. The sculptures give the room reason for being, but are perfectly attuned to its temporary and aspirational character. Along with the mosaics, they give the room the required 'representative character'—if the throne represents Honour, the sculpture represents Victory—but their material language questions the nature of that representation.

[20] Pagano also thought that Persico had overcome the *atteggiamenti polemici* (polemical attitudes) in so doing. From a privately printed 'Omaggio a Persico', not for commercial distribution, apparently to accompany the exhibition at the Galleria del Milione in May 1936, from the Leonardo Borgese Collection at the Getty Research Institute.

[21] 'In queste opere ogni esterna preoccupazione di stile è caduta, l'artista è cosi vivo da risolvere un motivo classico con la felicitá di un Lehmbruck o di un De Fiori…Questa è "l'impressionismo" di Fontana: la capacità dell'espressione viva e immediata.' 'Lucio Fontana II' (1935), Veronesi, op. cit., pp.189–90.

[22] This figure, coloured blue and gold, rejected from the exhibition, was intended for a blue space.

2.6   Lucio Fontana, *Vittoria dell'aria*, 1934, destroyed

SAARINEN'S CULTURE: CARL MILLES ON THE CRANBROOK CAMPUS (1934–42)

[1] A 1922 visit to the American Academy in Rome had provided the newspaper tycoon George Booth, who commissioned the project, with a model and a spur.

[2] A point of comparison, in terms of a project of similar scale and uniformity, and in progress in the same years, is the Vigeland Park in Oslo, which was being constructed throughout this period by the sculptor Gustav Vigeland (1869–1943). However, this space is a park—or indeed an early sculpture park—conceived in symbolist terms to represent man's journey through life and the architectural element is largely absent. Although the sculptures date largely to 1926–42, the majority was installed only after the sculptor's death.

In 1934, the Cranbrook Foundation, situated in the Bloomfield Hills north of Detroit, ordered forty-one sculptures (or sixty individual pieces) from the Swedish sculptor Carl Milles. Cranbrook was in the process of being developed as an educational campus. Since 1925, this project—which comprised both a physical infrastructure and an educational programme—had been directed by the Finnish architect Eliel Saarinen (1873–1950).[1] This situation presents two remarkable factors: the wholesale importation of a single sculptor's oeuvre, and the sculptures' placement in tandem with the construction of the buildings which they were to off-set.[2] Why, for a North American experimental community, does Saarinen choose so many ready-made works by one artist, and what does this tell us about the architect's attitude to sculpture?

Saarinen's career divides into two; the first part in Finland—initially with partners Gesellius and Lindgren, and then independently—the second part in America. From 1923, he was in Michigan, following his entry for the *Chicago Tribune* competition, and after a year teaching at the University of Michigan, the rest of his career was spent in Cranbrook. The Cranbrook project was the brainchild of the newspaper tycoon, George Booth, owner of the *Detroit News,* who was dedicated to the promotion of the Arts & Crafts ideal in the city and beyond. Booth met Saarinen in 1924, at the point when his impatience to see results meant that he was thinking of going beyond his previous more conventional beneficent activities. The career of Carl Milles (1875–1955) follows a similar pattern to that of Saarinen in dividing itself into Scandinavian and American halves. He had established himself rather successfully in his native Sweden with teaching and with public commissions prior to his arrival in Cranbrook.

Milles may have joined the teaching staff of the Cranbrook Academy in 1931, but this hardly explains why so much extant sculpture should be bought in one lot (for $120,000) and for a site that was still under construction. Even though he played hard to get, it is unlikely that the price of Milles' appointment was the purchase of so many of his works. But for an architect such as Eliel Saarinen—who not only designed the Cranbrook campus, but also established its educational ideal as being based on nurturing the different arts and crafts in a common environment—to choose

to buy a 'job-lot' seems especially surprising. Cranbrook had been set up as a place in which different kinds of artists worked together, finding new design solutions to specific physical requirements, on site. The purchase of all the sculpture in one fell swoop seems to make nonsense of this collaborative ideal.

In his later book *The Search for Form* (1948) Saarinen says little about sculpture explicitly, though he talks a good deal about the relationship between all the arts under the 'correlating wings' of architecture. This book only confirmed the approach which Saarinen had long advocated. In his early notes for the Cranbrook Foundation, for example, he talks repeatedly of the 'correlative environment', which he sees as equally important to the creative moment—'it is as necessary to create a proper environment for an art object as it is to create the object itself'—in order to argue for the integration of the junior and secondary

[3] Saarinen to the Cranbrook Foundation, 25/9/35. Archive references are to the Saarinen, Booth and Milles papers preserved in the Archive at Cranbrook (1981–01).

[4] The church was by Goodhue Associates, Brookside School by the Booth Family, and Cranbrook House and outbuildings by Albert Kahn. For a more detailed scheme see *Design in America*, Detroit Institute of Arts, 1983, p.351.

3.1   Paul Manship, *The Armillary Sphere*, 1924. Cranbrook School for Boys, Bloomfield Hills, Michigan

3.2   Carl Milles, *The Running Dogs*, 1910, Cranbrook, Bloomfield Hills, Michigan

schools with the Academy, and to provide a thorough context for art education.[3]

It is notable how the Cranbrook campus fulfils this aspiration, and how it was built in the order of a child's education, beginning with the church and the kindergarten, moving on to the primary and secondary schools, and then to the tertiary Art Academy. No works by Milles were added to either the church or the primary schools. They were, however, added to the boys' school (Cranbrook) and to the girls' school (Kingswood), which had also already been built. This means that no sculptures were added to any of the buildings by other architects, but only to buildings by Saarinen.[4]

In Cranbrook School, which opened in 1927, miscellaneous sculptural fragments (old and new) had been absorbed into the fabric of the buildings like so many aspects of an historic and picturesque site, employed in a discreet and largely informal manner. Their individual quality may not have been high, but cumulatively they gave character and particularity to the quadrangle (3.1). Milles' sculptures, which arrived later, were added at key points as punctuation, providing contrast (in the colour and finish of the bronze to the brick and stone around) and moments of almost colloquial intimacy. This is a collage of old and new, blended into a harmonious conversation piece, in which Milles' sculptures work as part of a vernacular stage set, designed for the pedestrian. They are never axial, nor frontal, but always liminal, on the edges of structures or tucked into corners, like pentimenti (3.2). They are small in scale, integrated unobtrusively and as if they 'belonged' to an old townscape.

The next major building project, Kingswood School for Girls (1931), which was also completed before Milles and his work arrived, afforded more limited scope to the placement of sculpture. Here, Saarinen had used the combined talents of his own family to create a fully integrated environment in all its architectural and decorative aspects, and alongside such richly inventive ironwork and carving (3.3) that one might well ask what place, if any, there was for sculpture. Milles' work is used more traditionally here than at Cranbrook School, in that it is given central and well-demarcated positions, at the ends of views or in the middle of interior courtyards. A few well-chosen pieces offset but also confirm the homogeneity

of the site, lifting and focusing views, adding notes of human movement and energy. That they are female sculptures—the earlier *Dancing Girls* (1914–17) and the *Diana* (1927)[5]—is surely not accidental (3.4).

When Saarinen does mention sculpture *per se*, he talks mainly about outdoor sculpture, its integration and its relationship to the environment and the weather. Milles' works are indeed disposed around the exterior environment of Cranbrook, despite the fact that, for Saarinen, the '"room" is the most indispensable form-problem'[6]. In Cranbrook we have the opportunity to study a room by Saarinen in almost complete original state, thanks to the recent restoration of his house. Sculpture itself has a very minor role here, although a small work by the Russian artist Mikhail Vrubel occupied a plinth in the sitting room, and a Waino Aaltonen figure was at the centre of the patio. These choices, if slight, would seem to be deliberate,

[5] One of the works which the American architects Holabird and Root had seen in Stockholm in the inner courtyard of the Swedish Match Company Building, and used again in one of their own interiors in Chicago.

[6] Eliel Sarinen, *The Search for Form*, 1985 edition, New York, p.127.

3.3   Eliel Saarinen, architectural detail—columns at Kingswood School, Cranbrook, Bloomfield Hills, Michigan

3.4   Reflection of Kingswood School, Cranbrook and Carl Milles, *Dancing Girls*, 1914–17

given the overall care with which the room has been put together, and lead one to surmise that Saarinen used these figurative sculptures to add notes of reflective interiority. They also added links to his own past, given that by 1925 Aaltonen was Finland's best-known sculptor, and that Finland was still culturally, if not politically, closely connected to Russia. Nevertheless, it seems clear that for Saarinen, the interior was reserved for a range of arts and crafts which effectively excluded the sculptor (but made use of the varied talents of his own family), and that the exterior was the sculptor's true territory.

An interesting 1934 carpet/map, designed by Eliel Saarinen and woven by his wife Loja, plots out the planned campus, built and unbuilt, and includes Milles' sculptures at the spots where they demarcate the different axes and entrances. On it can be identified

[7] *Design in America*, op cit, pp.243–4.

[8] This report comes from the Saarinen papers but its authorship is uncertain; it is described as 'Academy of Art—Original Plan' in the James S. Booth papers, Cyril Player draft (1990–08).

3.5   Cranbrook Academy of Art formal garden and pool, July 1935. Carl Milles' *Tritons* had recently been acquired by the Cranbrook Foundation. The formal garden was designed by Loja Saarinen

his *Europa and the Bull* at the head of the long pool bordered by five tritons on either side, with two terminating figures (probably *Sunglitter* and a centaur). Milles' *Orpheus Column* is to the right of *Europa*, and the *Jonah Fountain* is at the head of Academy Way, with two boars at the other end of the avenue. The Aaltonen figure is shown in Saarinen's garden, Milles' *Coursing Hounds* in the School, and another couple of pieces—including *Triton with Shell Fountain*—are placed in inner courtyards. Because all these sculptures were already extant, they served to characterise different areas of the master-plan, acting like sign-posts or literally as icons. That it clearly did not matter that they may have preceded the architecture itself would suggest that Saarinen saw sculpture's separateness from architecture as something distinctly positive.

Milles' *Orpheus Column* was already in place by 1930, and the *Jonah Fountain* by 1932.[7] In 1934, the bulk of his sculptures arrived, and both his *Triton* and *Orpheus* fountains were sited before the erection of what was to be their backdrop, for Saarinen's Museum and Library were only finished in 1941 (3.5). This in itself is remarkable, and photos from 1935 show the Triton sculptures apparently in place before the pool itself, and then, a little later, in their pool, still awaiting their architectural foil.

Photographs clearly reveal the vistas which came together with the completion of Cranbrook. The axes had been planned from the outset:

> The architect responsible for this tentative plan and model has captured with startling perception the character and contour of the ground, and has so attracted the elements to the axis that not one but many points reveal grave and charming collegiate vistas, each structure isolated by its natural and ordered park, and all linked by the natural alignment and grouping...[8]

Planning has delineated the internal crossroads, but planting has allowed the estate to sit within the wider landscape as if it had no borders. Looking out from the Museum steps down the Triton pool and into the trees, the grounds seem to extend infinitely. Saarinen's 1940 rendition of the Museum and Library gives an important place to the sculptures and totally ignores the planting which was soon to surround them

(3.6). Milles' sculptures confirmed these vistas through the later growth, and confirmed also how to read them. Cranbrook is an active campus as well as an estate, and these works help make the connections back into the centre. Sculptures are placed at its heart, not as eye-catchers on the limits of the campus, but closer to its architecture, as markers of creative and cultural space. On a campus, each of the components is both inward and outward-looking; self-centred, but part of a wider network or lineage. Smaller sculpture marks the interiority of individual courtyards, while the large works make links from one arena to the next. Sculptures signal the stages in the life of the community, coming together in smaller or larger numbers, and denote the transit from spaces of learning to places of leisure (3.7).

Cranbrook is its own little kingdom; sufficient unto itself, with an internal map that works primarily for its own citizens (educated within its walls), with sculptures marking their different rites of passage and their emergence onto the public stage. While the

[9] Loja mentions this in an undated note to George Booth (1981–01). The new Boymans van Beuningen was designed by Rotterdam's municipal architect A. van der Steur and opened on 6 July 1935.

3.6   Eliel Saarinen, *Cranbrook Academy of Art, perspective of the Museum and Library,* 1940. Pencil on illustration board

3.7   Cranbrook Academy of Art, Bloomfield Hills, Michigan. Carl Milles, *Sunglitter,* circa 1917

Cranbrook child has moved from nursery, to primary, to secondary, to tertiary education within this same campus, we move through an accelerated architectural history. We travel, across the space of its fifteen years as a construction site, from a layered and historicising recreation of a medieval European town centre, via a thorough re-working of the Scandinavian decorative aesthetic within an American Art Deco idiom, to a monumental vision which inserts itself into the context of other new buildings going up in Europe. Within the confines of Cranbrook itself, it is therefore possible to make various kinds of journey, each of which reveals chronology in a different way.

The Cranbrook Museum and Library is partly surprising because its peers are cultural buildings at the heart of major cities. It is clear that Saarinen was following the progress of contemporary museological projects in Europe, and indeed, on one of their regular return trips to Europe, he and Loja visited the new Boymans Museum in Rotterdam (where they liked the outside but not the inside arrangements).[9] Another major project to which the Cranbrook Museum and Library can again be compared is the Palais de Tokyo, erected in time for the 1937 Paris Exposition.[10] A further contemporary monumental project, more innovative in its approach, and of which both Saarinen and Milles were doubtless aware, was Erik Gunnar Asplund's Woodland Crematorium near Stockholm.[11] At the same time, moreover, both Eliel and Eero Saarinen were engaged in what was to be their winning submission for the Smithsonian Gallery of Art. This 1939 project, for a Federal site in central Washington, had no issue, and perhaps the Cranbrook Museum can be seen as a building which reflects that experience, despite its deeply rural setting.[12]

Sculpture is embedded in the Cranbrook journey. It goes from being part of an historic fabric, to being a figurative eye-catcher set high up or far off, to marking in its massing and positioning the public space of Cranbrook. This formality contrasts with the localised, intimate and largely informal encounters with single sculptures in and around the residential areas. The grand settings of the Museum and Library celebrate the coming-of-age of the Cranbrook student, and thus the transition from private to public space.

The most remarkable feature of the Museum and Library's composition is, however, the most under-stated. It is not the overall and impressive regularity of the frontal vista, but the irregular way in which smaller sculptures are displayed on the terrace and steps of the peristyle that joins the two buildings (3.8). Here the views are close-up and individualised rather than massed, and any engagement is up to the individual, for the experience is isolated, singular and ultimately unlocated. Though the grounds of Cranbrook can be understood as a classic landscape garden, using sculpture in both a formal (French) and informal (English) manner, the pavilion at its heart is unusual in the fact that the sculpture is absolutely non-axial, despite the frontality of its architectural surroundings. Throughout Cranbook, the sculpture is used outdoors, but it is when it most nearly enters the building that it become most interesting, and most unconventional.

These sculptures might ordinarily have been inside the Museum, on plinths or in vitrines, for they are part of its collection. Instead, they are arranged outside, on plinths designed to match the Museum doors,

[10] The Palais de Tokyo was planned by the curator of the Musée du Luxembourg, and designed by Aubert, Dastugue, Dondel and Viard.

[11] Asplund's Woodland Crematorium, on the southern outskirts of Stockholm, was designed by 1935 and finished by 1940. Its paved loggia was bordered by eight square columns on one length and six on the other, with John Lundqvist's bronze resurrection group placed within the forehall, but below an impluvium that breaks through the canopy. It is however a much lower building, and one set almost within the landscape rather than being raised up above it, as Saarinen's peristyle is, at least on one side. Milles had previously worked with Asplund on this site in supplying the *Angel of Death* for the roof of the Woodland Chapel (1918–20).

[12] The Smithsonian Gallery was one of the first Federal projects to be open to competition. Joseph Hudnut was invited to pick the jury, which included John A. Holabird, George Howe and Walter Gropius. The brief was for a 'dynamic' rather than a 'static museum of art', and thus the context was innovative in most respects other than the site. See E.G. Grossman, *The Civic Architecture of Paul Cret*, Cambridge, 1996, pp.201–11.

[13] The work of one other sculptor is set on a pedestal on the Museum steps: Marshall Fredericks, Milles' assistant and a long-time teacher at Cranbrook.

[14] Note that Le Corbusier and Robert Mallet-Stevens had also produced schemes for the competition for the 'Musées de la Ville et de l'Etat à Paris'.

3.8   Cranbrook Art Museum, main entrance

effectively turning the building inside out, or playing on its seemingly monolithic character by suggesting that its collection has escaped (3.9). Set intimately and carefully in relation to its viewer, as it is by the architect, the sculpture is allowed once again to be an artwork. Milles is thus closely associated with, and perhaps clarifies the ultimate goal of, the Cranbrook scheme: he is the artist, his work is the collection. Milles' work is the art which Saarinen's museum extols.[13] The artist—when all is said and done—is removed from the architect and from the designer; a purveyor of different gifts.

The Palais de Tokyo, erected for the 1937 Exposition Internationale in Paris, had always been intended to survive the fair and to become a modern art museum for the collections of both the city and the state.[14] Its sculptural scheme, though extensive, is extremely traditional, carried out by a number of sculptors but within a common figurative norm, employing a bland classicising style that gains its effect from the massing and repetition of standing female figures and relief sculpture.[15] It is against an example such as this that Saarinen's use of Milles' sculpture, above all on the steps of his Museum peristyle, shows its originality. Where the Palais de Tokyo is homogenous, in style and material, Cranbrook is about contrast. The Paris museum reads from afar, but close up becomes less interesting; Cranbrook is the opposite. With one eye on the 'modern art museum', Saarinen's Library and Museum are also full of an idiosyncratic, almost Rococo, attention to detail which draws on both the Oriental and the Aztec. The approach to decorative detailing that is so rewarding in this seemingly monumental building carries through to the sculpture. Contrary to expectation, the sculpture is not 'applied' for effect. Indeed, it is not applied at all. Neither relief, nor architectural, nor decorative, this sculpture is given its own—sculptural—space (3.10).

Why did Saarinen use Milles—and so much of Milles? Despite Cranbrook's ostensible purpose as a place of creative production, Saarinen clearly preferred to work with pieces that he could assess in advance. The sculpture helps us to remember the architecture, and to remember what it signifies. It furnishes or expresses the meanings of its constituent parts, taken in isolation or together. Works by one sculptor are used in relation to the works of one architect. If the architecture changed more radically over time, the sculpture nevertheless embodied the same time-line, since Milles' early works pre-dated the latest by some twenty years. The homogeneity of the sculpture means that it might sometimes go unnoticed, but also that it functions throughout according to its own consistent register. It is showy when it needs to be showy, quiet when it needs to be quiet. Sculpture joins up the campus and sets the pace of the overall experience. Sculpture played no part in the interior; it was different, and it was placed outdoors. The purchase of forty pieces gave Saarinen a secure and constant language with which to articulate the site according to the original master plan.[16]

The role of Milles' sculpture in relation to Saarinen's architecture is highly unusual. Whereas it is commonplace for sculpture to be placed after the architecture is designed, at Cranbrook, it often comes before the buildings. This might lead us to conclude that the

[15] See P. Curtis, *Sculpture 1900–1945,* Oxford, 1999, pp.236–7.

[16] The original master plan was very much a work of collaboration between George Booth and Saarinen. It should be pointed out that Milles had designed his own sculpture garden, at his house in Lidingo, in Stockholm, between 1906 and 1929, and he continued to embellish it up until his death.

3.9   Cranbrook Art Museum. Marshall Fredericks, *The Thinker,* 1940

Saarinen's Culture

[17] Nevertheless, Eames worked with Milles on his St Louis fountain project, and Milles' design for the *Good Father in Heaven* (1946) would seem to influence Eero in his submission for the Jefferson National Expansion Memorial (the Gateway Arch) (1947). A more well-publicised similarity was with Adalberto Libera's design for the Esposizione Universale di Roma (planned for 1942) and for its promotional material.

3.10 Cranbrook Art Museum. Carl Milles, *Horse's Head*

sculpture is conceived of by the architect as entirely separate—and thus secondary in importance—or, on the contrary, as entirely separate and thus, in some ways at least, as primary. In either case, it seems clear that sculpture stood apart from the design vision for which Cranbrook became famous. Some of the students closest to Milles at Cranbrook—Harry Bertoia, Charles Eames and Saarinen's son Eero—rejected sculpture as a discipline, and effectively underlined its shortcomings by what they did in the field of design.[17] Their work was a much more fitting manifestation of the ideas which Cranbrook had been set up to nurture. Nevertheless, it is apparent (even if never explicitly stated) that the Cranbrook ideal—as developed by Saarinen, and played out by Milles—was absolutely ready to allow sculpture a separate space. The campus itself reveals the truth of the accusation that the departments of sculpture and architecture were indeed the prestige departments, and shows that Saarinen needed Milles just as Milles needed Saarinen. If Saarinen's deference might be understood as a symptom—if not a cause—of sculpture's increasing irrelevance, it might also be read as a revealing indication of the real limits of the arts and crafts programme.

PAPER VISIONS: 'NEW BUILDINGS FOR 194X' (1943)

1 *The Architectural Forum,* May 1943. Mies' project is on pp.84–5.

2 'Nine Points on Monumentality' (1943), in S. Giedion, *architecture, you and me,* Cambridge, Mass., 1958, pp.48–51.

In May 1943, *The Architectural Forum* published an article, presented as one in a series of occasional features. Titled 'New Buildings for 194X', it represented twenty-three projects for a 'hypothetical town of 70,000', but has principally become famous for just one entry: Mies van der Rohe's Museum. Two plans —a city plan, and another of the town centre— showed where the various projects were in relation to one another. Mies' Museum was on one side of a square bordered by the City Hall, the bank and an office building, each of them presented individually in the larger scheme. Some well-known architects, including Louis Kahn, Charles Eames, Holabird and Root, William Lescaze and Serge Chermayeff were also featured, but Mies' project is often discussed as if it stood alone.[1]

The simplicity (in keeping with that alloted to each of the featured architects) of Mies' double-page black and white spread—with reproductions of one sketch, one plan, and two collages—belies its far-reaching effect (4.1). In his short accompanying text, Mies made a number of points. He stressed that this museum was for a small city and not for a metropolis. His (somewhat unexpected) corollary was that the collection must thus be of a high quality and well displayed. To make the museum a 'center for the enjoyment, not the interment of art', Mies proposes a 'garden approach to the display of sculpture'. In this way, 'Interior sculptures enjoy an equal spatial freedom, because the open plan permits them to be seen against the surrounding hills. The architectural space, thus achieved, becomes a defining rather than a confining space'.

It is worth placing Mies' 'garden approach' in the context of the debate on the 'new monumentality' which was first articulated in the same year. In their 'Nine Points on Monumentality', J.L. Sert, Fernand Léger and Sigfried Giedion opined that 'the people want the buildings that represent their social and community life to give more than functional fulfilment'. They added that, 'The following conditions are essential for it: A monument, being the integration of the work of the planner, architect, painter, sculptor, and landscapist, demands close collaboration between all of them.'[2]

The monument in itself is not exactly defined, but would appear to derive from the right combination of

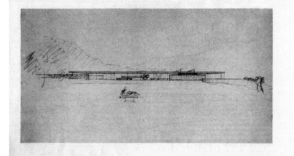

circumstances around it. Above all it needs to be in the right place, for it requires open space, and is made complete by trees, plants and water.

Sert, Léger and Giedion had originally met in 1943 in order to discuss their individual contributions to an article to be published by the American Abstract Artists, but instead decided to pool their ideas. As the publication was delayed, Giedion's own contribution was in fact published first, in Paul Zucker's 1944 anthology *New Architecture and City Planning*, and some of its passages are also to be found in the 'Nine Points'. In this, Giedion makes it clear that whereas modern architecture in the States had been largely confined to domestic or industrial buildings, in other countries it had moved into the field of 'museums, theatres, universities, churches or concert halls', and that in such cases it had been forced to 'seek the monumental expression'.[3] If we see the museum as

[3] S. Giedion, 'The Need for a New Monumentality', in P. Zucker (ed.), *New Architecture and City Planning*, New York, 1944, p.552.

[4] Ibid., p.553.

[5] 'New Buildings for 194X', *The Architectural Forum* (New York), May 1943, p.84.

[6] *The Architectural Review* (London), September 1948, pp.117–128. The architects were Gregor Paulsson, Henry-Russell Hitchcock, William Holford, Sigfried Giedion, Walter Gropius, Lucio Costa and Alfred Roth. According to Giedion, the symposium was the result of a lecture given at the RIBA on 26 September 1946. See his *architecture, you and me*, op. cit., p.23.

4.1   *Architectural Forum*, May 1943, pages 84–85

one of the first examples of the new monumentality, and if we recognise the proximity of Mies' statement to that of Giedion, we see how we have arrived at the point where art and architecture mesh extremely closely.

Giedion defines the need for monumentality as the need 'of the people to own symbols which reveal their inner life, their actions and their social conceptions'.[4] He wants the monument to be a community centre in the sense of the agora, forum or square. He notes that symbolism does occur in temporary spectacles and manifestations (his focus on the pavilion was probably influenced by his experience of recent World Fairs), but needs to be integrated in more permanent form within the civic centre. Similarly, Mies talks of his project as 'providing a noble background for the civic and cultural life of the whole community'.[5] What might such definitions mean for the art that is housed in the Museum for a Small City? Is it more or less symbolic than the building itself, and how might it help to create shared spaces?

In September 1948, the *Architectural Review* (London) published 'In Search of a New Monumentality': 'a symposium by' seven leading architects.[6] Their views were summarised and compared in the prefatory remarks. It was assumed that all departed from the same premise: that the modern idiom, being based on functionalism, was insufficiently expressive. Representational buildings—'town halls, cinemas, sports arenas, public libraries'—will again be required, and in them 'the community calls for some kind of monumental gesture'. The terms adopted by most of the discussants seem to take us some way from the 'Nine Points', and the durability, solidity and dignity that the architect Henry-Russell Hitchcock takes as givens are contested by Gropius and Giedion. Sincerity and sentiment are invoked by all, but defined differently. Genuine monumentality is understood to be unconscious in its own time, which means that the industrial infrastructure may well provide vehicles of monumental expression. But such structures are utilitarian, as well as massive and durable, and so we are brought back to the nub of the problem. In this symposium, which united dissenting voices, monumentality is not necessarily desirable, for it may, to some, be inextricably linked with totalitarianism. The nearest the contributors come to consensus, or

to conclusion, is that a new monumentality will embrace landscape and city planning, and the incorporation of natural elements such as trees and rocks.

Let us return to Mies' 'garden approach' to the museum. There is another parallel between the views of Mies and Giedion, for both speak of the museum as a prison. Giedion talks of art being banished to museums and kept there 'behind bolts and bars'[7] and Mies of wishing to avoid the usual 'interment of art'. Giedion notes that art rarely escapes the luxury bracket, but his exception is Pablo Picasso's *Guernica*, 'ordered by the Spanish Loyalist Government'[8]. In his collage for the museum (which is right at the heart of the hypothetical city), Mies shows four sculptures and two paintings, one of which is *Guernica* (4.2).

[7] S. Giedion (1958), op. cit., p.24.

[8] P. Zucker, op. cit., p.557.

[9] Picasso had been asked to execute a large painting for the pavilion in January 1937, well before the bombing of Guernica in late April. This event spurred him to begin planning what was to become *Guernica*. In the Spanish Pavilion, its context was a combination of art—five sculptures by Picasso, one by Alberto Sanchez, and one by Julio Gonzalez, a mural by Joan Miró, the fountain by Calder—and of documentary photography and graphics. The pavilion opened a month after the Exposition was inaugurated and closed in November. *Guernica* toured Scandinavia and then Britain in 1938. It arrived in New York in May 1939, and was exhibited in aid of Spanish refugees

in New York, Los Angeles, San Francisco and Chicago. In late 1939 it joined the major Picasso retrospective at MoMA, which later travelled to Chicago. MoMA looked after the painting for the duration of the war, though it travelled occasionally within the States, and more widely thereafter, and ultimately the loan was extended until 1981.

4.2   Ludwig Mies van der Rohe, 'Museum for a Small City Project' interior perspective 1941–3. Cut-out photographs and photographic reproductions on illustration board, 77.5 x 102.9 cm. MoMA, New York

4.3   Patio-Auditorium by J. L. Sert, Spanish Pavilion, 1937, Exposition internationale des arts et techniques, Paris

The painting had already been shown in a gallery space that did not simply resemble a pavilion in its architecture, but was officially so. It was painted for the Pavilion of the Spanish Republican Government at the 1937 Exposition internationale, Paris.[9] There, it was described as a mural, and indeed occupied most of one wall at the right side of the entrance space, a space which was open at its sides, but protected from above by a second floor (4.3). It was fronted by the fountain which Calder made from mercury, which was a literal replacement for the more usual Mercury Fountain. The pavilion was designed by Sert, one of Giedion's co-authors. In one of the post-war discussions held by CIAM (Congrès Internationaux d'Architecture Moderne) about the connections between the plastic arts, Sert described his experience of that conjunction:

It was working in that pavilion, a place of public assembly, that I realized the importance of placing works of art in places where many people gather together, and that, in these places, they form an indispensable complement to the architecture. Unfortunately we have today very little opportunity of finding places of this sort, and for this reason we have today quite a different conception of the place of sculpture in our towns.[10]

A few months after the publication of 'New Buildings for 194X' in the New York *Architectural Forum*, Ray Eames published a short piece about her art in the Californian magazine *Arts & Architecture*.[11] Charles Eames had joined the Board of this magazine in February 1942, and Ray joined the Advisory Board the

[10] J.L. Sert in 'Architects and Politics: An East-West Discussion' (CIAM 8, Bergamo, 1949) in S. Giedion, 1958, op. cit., p.81.

[11] September issue, pp.16–17.

[12] Entenza was the publisher and editor of the magazine from 1938 to 1962.

[13] F.Schulze, *Philip Johnson, Life and Work*, New York, 1994, p.175.

4.4   Photo-collage by Ray Eames for artist's statement, published in *Arts and Architecture*, September, 1943

following May, when her design of Californian coastal defences was featured on the cover. The magazine as a whole, containing the invective of John Entenza's editorials,[12] combined with the copious pleas to buy war bonds, and adverts for plywood furniture and pre-fabricated homes, reminds one of the context in which the Eames were developing. (The term 194X was itself a commonly used signifier for the year when the war would end.) Inside the September 1943 issue was a collage by Ray Eames, on a double-page spread which also featured text and two paintings. Not only has the collage itself been isolated from the other components that made up this spread, but the article as a whole is rarely situated within the context of Entenza's war-time ire. His scathing remarks about war-mongerers and profiteers give relevance to the collage, which includes pictures of parachutes, soldiers, military installations and a plane. Among this military hardware, Eames includes Picasso's *Guernica* (4.4).

Guernica was by this time in America, where it had toured extensively and was now in the care of the Museum of Modern Art. It had thus become not just a public painting, but a virtually American painting, and was therefore closely associated in the American context with the possibility of the 'new monumentality'. Developing his plans for an exhibition of memorial buildings at MoMA, or for a book, Philip Johnson wrote to Mies in the autumn of 1945:

> I have been trying strenuously to put across the idea that you should build in our garden [at the museum] a pavilion to house 'Guernica'. Unfortunately I can not get any money... My hope is this, that you can design a pavilion for, let us say, Lincoln Park or some appropriate site in Chicago... I would like to show these designs by means of your perspectives, with 'Guernica' montaged on them.[13]

The actual war-time circuit of *Guernica* within America, along with its virtual imposition into the spaces of other writers, artists and architects—montaged onto Giedion's text, Eames' collage, Johnson's plans—explains how the painting might become a tool in an argument. In using *Guernica* in his own museum project, Mies shows that he is not simply topical, but public too. His collage—his superimposition of existing works of art into his own, non-existent space—is a

statement about the meaning of public life. And the placement of a work such as *Guernica*, as both Mies and Johnson realised, was important. The pavilion was the building type that best represented the desired openness. It was also a form that made fewer claims to permanence.

Most prominent in Ray Eames' collage—more prominent than *Guernica*—is Lehmbruck's *Kneeling Woman* (1911). Just as Mies juxtaposed his *Guernica* with a crouching female sculpture, so Eames showed a sorrowing 'commemorative' figure. The sculptures assert the meaning of the painting, standing in for us and for a common response. These are works closely associated with loss in war. *Kneeling Woman* was to be incorporated by Mies into his later plans for Houston and for Berlin, but in the 1943 *Architectural Forum* he uses only works by Maillol. Mies had been

[14] Later to be replaced (by Mary Callery) with an image of an Egyptian scribe (probably in an Alinari reproduction of a piece in the Louvre). Peter Behrens had used the same Maillol (in a plaster version) as the centrepiece of his Exhibition Hall ('Raum 15') at the 1907 Mannheim Kunst-und-Gartenbau-Ausstellung.

[15] Detailed in Neil Levine's '"The Significance of Facts": Mies' Collages Up Close and Personal' in *Assemblage*, no. 37, December 1998.

4.5   Ludwig Mies van der Rohe, *Project for Concert Hall Collage,* 1942 (second version). Collage over photograph, (75 x 157.5 cm). MoMA, New York

including real sculptures by Lehmbruck and Kolbe since the late 1920s, as we have seen. Maillol seems to join them in the early 1930s, in sketch form at first. The first Maillol sculpture to enter Mies' space in collage form appears in the Concert Hall collage of 1942, which is less obviously a space for art.[14] Here, his *Mediterranean* of 1905 was added to the collage that had as its background Albert Kahn's Aircraft Assembly Plant, recently built and published.[15] *Mediterranean* added a small, brooding presence to the vast empty space, somehow suggesting that all is not what it seems (4.5).

It was in the 1930s that Mies had begun to use collages as a way of presenting his work, and his students are known to have helped him in their construction. The collage approach for the inclusion of existing works of art makes very obvious sense with presentations

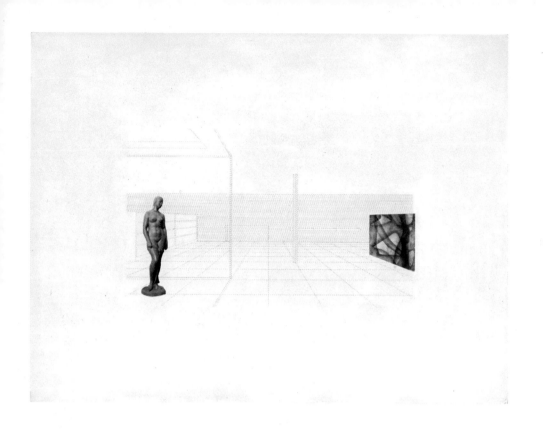

[16] A. Drexler, MVDR Archive 690.63, dated to 1931 in Drexler, but to 1938 by Andres Lepik in his essay on 'Mies and Photomontage' in the 2003 exhibition catalogue, *Mies in Berlin*. Drexler dates the sculpture to 1919, but it is 1910.

[17] A. Drexler: 994.65 and 458.64.

[18] 'Bunte Mahlzeit' ('Colourful Meal / Gay Repast / A Motley Meal'), 1928, was owned by Mrs Stanley Resor (one of Mies' clients) after 1937. See C. Giedion-Welcker's 1951 monograph on Klee, p.143. This work was borrowed from Mrs Resor to be included in the Paul Klee Memorial Exhibition at the Arts Club of Chicago in February 1941, along with over eighty other pieces.

[19] Braque was the subject of a large exhibition (with sixty-eight works) at the Arts Club of Chicago in November 1939, one of a series of retrospective exhibitions of European masters which Mies would probably have seen.

[20] This 'Study' was included in the Maillol exhibition at the Arts Club of Chicago in December 1940. Alongside the twenty-five sculptures, seven studio photographs were also included. 'Night' was shown on the cover of the souvenir catalogue.

4.6 Ludwig Mies van der Rohe, Row House with Interior Court project. Interior perspective after 1938. MoMA, New York. Collage of cut-and-pasted reproductions on illustration board, (76.2 x 101.6 cm)

4.7 Ludwig Mies van der Rohe, Court House project after 1938. Interior perspective. MoMA, New York. Graphite and cut-and-pasted reproduction (of unidentified sculpture) on illustration board, (76.2 x 101.6 cm)

for art galleries, but in fact the first instance in Mies' work occurs in relation to projects for court houses, or houses with interior courts. The first instance is probably Lehmbruck's *Standing Female Figure* (1910), which appears in his court-house collage of 1931–8 (4.6).[16] Another, perhaps classical, standing female figure appears in two further court house collages dated to c. 1934 (4.7).[17]

Although only two collages were illustrated in *The Architectural Forum*, Mies and his assistants had made one or two others as alternatives. Of the three preserved at MoMA, only one (724.63) is reproduced in the magazine. Another (723.63) has the same sculptures as the upper illustration in the spread, but replaces the painting by Paul Klee[18] with a detail of a Braque.[19] The third piece (995.65) shows a different combination of the same artworks that feature in the magazine, now placing Maillol's reclining figure in front of *Guernica* and *Action in Chains* striding towards us.

It is notable that Mies uses only Maillol (whereas a more likely museum display would mix a wider range of artworks) and that he puts Maillol with Picasso. If we were to look for what the sculptures—*Night*, *Action in Chains*, *Torso* and *Study for the Monument to Cézanne*[20]—had in common (other than their author) we might discern that they all seem to turn away from us. *Action in Chains* and the reclining study are also monumental works, in that they commemorate the departed: Auguste Blanqui and Paul Cézanne, respectively. *Action in Chains* shows a woman freed of her chains and commemorates a notable Socialist activist who had spent half his life in jail. Both were monuments rejected by the communities that had commissioned them and were subsequently the subject of long campaigns for their recognition. (The *Monument to Cézanne*, commissioned for Aix-en-Provence in 1912, was only finally erected in Paris in 1929.) *Night*, in which a female seems to bury her face, has much of the quality of a tomb sculpture. The combination of these sculptures with *Guernica* cannot be accidental; whether they walk away or bury their face in their arms, the figures in these sculptures are responding to catastrophe.

Mies used the same medium and the same vocabulary in his later projects for art galleries. From 1954, he worked on the Addition to the Cullinan Hall for the

Houston Museum of Fine Arts. When the Cullinan Hall was opened in autumn 1958, it was expected that the new wing and the sculpture garden would follow shortly.[21] A collage for the 'terrace and sculpture garden', presented to the Trustees in 1958, sets four sculptures in front of the existing trees, while adding paving, a small marble wall and a low pool.[22] They recede in space, giving a shallow area greater depth, as does the paving, but they also provide greater poignancy. The three European sculptures— Lehmbruck's *Kneeling Woman* and his *Fallen*, and Maillol's *Mountain* (1937) look down in states of utter stillnesss. They are enclosed, introverted and at rest. The Asian Buddha is similarly fixed. The impression conveyed is of a memorial garden (or cemetery) as much as of a place of leisure or aesthetic appreciation. And indeed, perhaps it is not untrue to say that for Mies, his use of Lehmbruck, the friend who had taken his own life in 1919 at the age of thirty-eight, was always commemorative (4.8).[23]

The Cullinan Hall in Houston was a remarkable space of ample dimensions, described as an open court, but most reminiscent of a theatre auditorium in its fan-like shape. It was one space, two-storeys high —110 x 95 feet with a ceiling 32 feet high—enclosing 10,000 square feet. Mies knew that the hall was only one step in the Museum of Fine Art's more extensive building programme, seeing it as firstly a multi-purpose space, and later on, a central core that 'could then be used for, perhaps, sculpture'.[24] The building committee, uncertain about the proposals, was told that it might gain 'a heroic monument, a great exhibition hall'. It was a space that needed to be installed in a certain way, for with its enormous span, high white walls and polished floor (of dark green terrazzo), it needed anchoring at its centre. Sculpture did this most effectively, and its impact was most obvious at night, when the huge gallery facade, lit up inside, converted the sculptures' textures into simple silhouettes. This was not just a collage brought to life, but also echoed with its large-screen, night-time spectacle the visions of the 'new monumentality'.

The Cullinan's inaugural exhibition— *The Human Image* — was designed by Mies, with installations by David Haid and Gene Summers, his assistants. They set up long, low white screens for the paintings,

[21] The Brown Wing was opened in 1974, after Mies' death. See also M. Brawne, *The New Museum*, London, 1965 for Mies' Houston and Berlin projects. The Cullen Sculpture Garden was ultimately designed by Isamu Noguchi between 1976 and 1984.

[22] Schulze and Danforth, MVDR Archive, 5405B.87. The landscape architect Thomas Church had prepared an earlier plan, which also transformed the south lawn while retaining the existing trees.

[23] Perhaps one might see his use of Klee in a similar way, given that his favourite painter had died in 1940, and that Mies had quite actively acquired his work in the last two years of his life. There is an added poignancy (intentional or not) in his use of German artists then defined as 'degenerate' by the National Socialist Party.

[24] Stephen Fox, 'An architectural history of the museum 1924–1953', *Museum of Fine Arts, Special Bulletin*, Houston, 1991, vol.15, no.1, p.74.

[25] Lee Malone, foreword for the commemorative catalogue for the opening of Cullinan Hall, *The Human Image*, 10 October–23 November, 1958, n.p.

4.8 Ludwig Mies van der Rohe, Cullinan Wing Addition. The Museum of Fine Arts, Houston, Texas. Perspective of terrace and sculpture garden, 1954. MoMA, New York. Ink and photographic collage on illustration board, (76.2 x 101.6 cm)

and large white pedestals which accommodated several of the smaller sculptures. The exhibits on loan, which ranged from 'The Ancient Image' to the recent past, presented 'enduring concepts of style in the human form'. In the twentieth-century selection were included sculptures by Maillol, Brancusi, Lehmbruck, Giacometti, Moore and Smith. The Director's foreword gives a good feel for the underlying 'meaning' of the show: 'Through the contemplation of the human figure, he [man] continuously returns to such lasting and absorbing relationships as man and woman, man and his social and natural environment, man and his awareness of death and of divinity.'[25]

The Human Image was much less well received than

the next exhibition, which was guest-curated by Jermayne MacAgy. *Totems not Taboo* used sculpture to even greater effect to anchor the Cullinan Hall, which must have seemed at times like an enormous tent or canopy which might lift off into space. In 1961, the well-known curator, J.J. Sweeney, arrived as the Museum of Fine Arts' new director, and he not only picked up on Mies' design solutions, but went further, by abandoning the screens and literally suspending the paintings in mid-air. Mies was impressed by the photographic documentation that he was sent. (Sweeney's taste in art also echoed Mies', being fundamentally rooted in, by now classic, modernist masters.) Suspended paintings provided the unfixed screen against which people and sculptures could be positioned. The paintings hang in the air, reflecting in the terrazzo like a moving chequerboard, while the sculptures are rooted to the ground. Sweeney's installations enjoyed a symbiotic relationship with Mies' collages, and they seem to be the only actual installations that lived up to the imagery employed in Mies' original design.

The collage and drawing combination is extremely effective for the presentation of sculpture in modernist architecture: solid cut-out sculptures (their thickness palpable in the original collages)[26] are set against planar screens of foliage or water, as well as against paintings, within an airy framework of ruled lines, marking out the receding tiles of the floor, the windows and screens behind the works. Set against a long horizontal band, they are rarely delimited at their sides, as if the space might flow endlessly from left to right. The striding quality of *Action in Chains* in the 1943 Museum project enhances this feeling of a moving screen passing behind the object. Here we might once again refer to the tract on the 'new monumentality', which emphasises this very aspect. In their ninth point, the authors suggest that its effects are not fixed: it would change according to the available light, and might include mobile or changing elements projected onto its new large planar surfaces. This 'new and vast facade' might extend 'for many miles'.[27]

The vocabulary made manifest in the Museum project of 1943 was one of great continuity and sufficiency for Mies, who used it over a thirty-year period. It worked for him and for his architecture. It also sets up a combination that we see used again—explictly or

[26] Ursel Berger has identified the source of the Maillol photographs in John Rewald's 1939 monograph.

[27] Giedion (1958), op. cit., p.51.

4.9   Ludwig Mies van der Rohe, Collage for the Neue Nationalgalerie Berlin, 1960, 75.5 x 101.5 cm, Nationalgalerie, Staatliche Museen zu Berlin

4.10   Ludwig Mies van der Rohe, Collage for the Neue Nationalgalerie Berlin, 1960, 75.5 x 101.5 cm, Nationalgalerie, Staatliche Museen zu Berlin

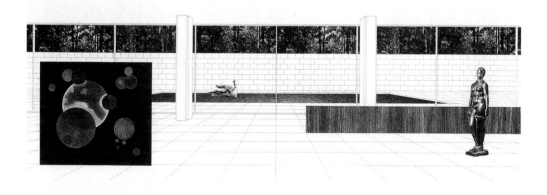

Paper Visions

[28] Getty Research Institute, Special Collections, 2003.R.21.

[29] This work is not catalogued by Schulze and Danforth, but is reproduced by M. Vandenberg in his monograph on the gallery (1998), fig. 38, in a photograph from Hedrich Blessing.

4.11   Neue Nationalgalerie, Berlin, showing Wilhelm Lehmbruck's *Thinker,* 1913–4

implicitly—by many other architects, and none more obviously than Philip Johnson at the Museum of Modern Art. In Johnson's case, however, he uses real sculptures as if they were collaged images, and it is conceivable that Mies, in turn, borrowed from Johnson in the placing of the real sculptures in his plans for the Berlin New National Gallery (opened 1968). Their arrangement in relation to the sculpture terrace and pool is, above all, remarkably similar (4.9, 4.10). Presentation photographs of collages for Berlin show Lehmbruck's *Kneeling Woman* with a Kandinsky, and his 1910 *Standing Female Figure* in front of a long, oblong pool with Maillol's *River* toppling in, just as in MoMA.[28] Another collage shows Auguste Renoir's *Washerwoman* to the left of *Guernica*, and Mies' 'favourite' Lehmbruck torso (*Woman Looking Back* of 1913–4) to the right.[29] (The Renoir was ultimately placed outside, alongside the pool, in a manner very similar to its position at MoMA.) Lehmbruck's *Thinker* (1913–4) is sited indoors, but on the grand upper gallery, which is to all intents and purposes, an outdoor space (4.11).

Philip Johnson's 'outdoor room' at the Museum of Modern Art belongs in the discussion of the 'new monumentality' just as much as Mies' Museum for a Small City. It is easier to understand Johnson's sculpture garden in this broad sense than in terms of its sculptures. The formal links with Mies are clear, and most obviously in the collage-like effect to which sculpture is central. The sculpted human figure (generally female) punctuates and articulates a blank open space broken up by occasional blocks and screens. The figures reveal its spatial layering, almost as if they were in a model theatre. The extra-formal role of the sculpture is, however, obscure. If it is used because it is 'significant', what does it signify? The space is as much about leisure as study. Do the sculptures reveal the inner life of the people who encounter them, or are they simply the old-fashioned excuses for a new 'monumental' space that has little to do with them? If the sculptures are speaking softly, what do they say?

JOHNSON'S
FIXING:
THE MoMA
SCULPTURE
GARDEN (1953)

[1] Her 1939 gift included a number of works by each of the following sculptors: Despiau, Kolbe, Lachaise, Lehmbruck and Maillol. Mrs Rockefeller was also working throughout this period with the landscape architect Beatrix Farrand on the grounds of her estate at Seal Harbor in Maine, designed to show Mrs Rockefeller's collection of oriental sculpture.

[2] Or cryptomeria, hornbeam and weeping birch, according to the source.

[3] Hilary Lewis and John O'Connor, *Philip Johnson: The architect in his own words,* New York, 1994, p.67. Note also Johnson's 1965 essay 'Whence and Whither: The Processional Element of Architecture', which emphasises the temporal aspects of architectural experience.

5.1 (following page) Philip Johnson, The Abby Aldrich Rockefeller Sculpture Garden. North view. MoMA, New York, 1953. Photographed 1953 by Alexander Georges PA485

In 1953, New York's Museum of Modern Art opened its new sculpture garden, designed by Philip Johnson (1906–2005) (5.1). The sculptures on display were among the exhibits from the exhibition *Sculpture of the 20th Century*. In this, it was following a precedent. The first Museum garden, dating back to 1939, and designed by Alfred Barr with John McAndrew, had similarly been inaugurated in conjunction with a major loan exhibition—*Art in Our Time*—and about twenty of its sixty sculpture exhibits were positioned out of doors. The first garden was named after Abby Aldrich Rockefeller, whose planned gift to the Museum of thirty-six sculptures[1] gave it ample reason for being. Her death in 1948 provided another fitting reason for its renovation.

Johnson's lineage, in terms of his indebtedness to Mies, is clearly manifested in the 1952–3 design. Its use of fine materials in making a secluded sunken space, which is as much a room as a garden, despite its oblong pools, makes palpable links with Mies' Barcelona pavilion, which Johnson had recently documented with life-size montages in his 1947 Mies exhibition at MoMA. The MoMA garden was 200 feet long by 175 feet wide, lined with substantial slabs of Vermont marble, with a floor level about 3 feet below that of the museum. The space was bisected by a 'canal', which was staggered by pulling two sections apart, and then divided into four by the addition of two footbridges. The delicately graphic trees—weeping beech, birch, andromedas and poplars[2]—emerging out of low patches of foliage, acted like little groves that broke up the garden with their tracery, bridging the solidity of the sculpture and the blankness of the backdrop. Early photographs show how light and thin these trees originally were, in comparison to their later growth. The planting was designed to encourage the user to take an indirect route around the garden and to encounter the sculptures from different angles.

In a later book of interviews, Johnson asserts: 'this is a room, not a garden. It's an urban room with definite doorways and processionals. And yet it's easy enough to penetrate. If you're not forced to move that way and this way, you won't see anything.'[3]

The hard structure is absolutely rectilinear, and though the garden was indeed often described as an 'outdoor

Johnson's Fixing

The MoMA Sculpture Garden

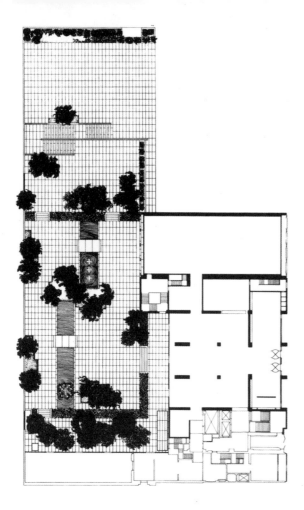

room', it might be better described in the plural, since the ground-plan (5.2) suggests a house with several rooms. This effect was enhanced by the fact that the north wall, bordering the street, was 14 feet high, and thus akin to the height of a ceiling in a single-storey modernist house. The whole, moreover, was inserted into existing urban fabric, and was more like a building lot bordered by walls than a 'land-scaped' garden in the usual sense.

In *The Architectural Review* of September 1950, Johnson had explicitly presented his house at New Canaan (5.3) as derivative, numbering Mies as one of several sources.[4] While the idea of the glass house may have come from Mies (who was then engaged on building the Farnsworth House), as did the arrangement

[4] Historians have since questioned Johnson's suggested analysis and have put more emphasis on his own process, which lasted from 1945 to 1947. See S. Jenkins and D. Mohney in *The Houses of Philip Johnson*, New York, 2001, p.64, where they quote Frampton's 1978 description of the process as being about resolving the 'courthouse/belvedere conflict'. Scheme XXVII, of November 1947, shows both the plinth for the sculpture and the screen for the painting (p.87).

[5] In 1962, below the Glass House, floating on the pond, Johnson built a pavilion, based proportionally on the dwarf's quarters in the Ducal Palace at Mantua. Registering as a full-scale building from a distance, but gradually shrinking as one approached, it was in fact only 6 feet high.

[6] Philip Johnson, 'House at New Canaan, Connecticut', *The Architectural Journal*, September 1950, p.159.

[7] The early 'Man in the Open Air' (c.1915) was gifted to MoMA, New York in 1948 and put in the sculpture garden. By 1954, MoMA had eight sculptures by Nadelman.

5.2   Philip Johnson, The Abby Aldrich Rockefeller Sculpture Garden, plan

5.3   Philip Johnson, Glass House, New Canaan, Connecticut, 1950, showing Elie Nadelman's *Two Circus Women*, c1930, in background

of the units, Johnson also underlined the eighteenth-century precedents in the house's siting.[5] He mentioned two other aspects that he owed to Mies: the furniture, and the notion of the sculpture group: (5.4) 'The papier-mâché group by Nadelman provides the type of foil which this kind of building needs (Mies again established the precedent in his Barcelona Pavilion).'[6]

Elie Nadelman had died at the end of 1946, and in 1948, MoMA presented a memorial exhibition of his work, making amends, perhaps, for its earlier neglect.[7] The work that was to become Johnson's—the 5-foot high *Two Circus Women*—was reproduced as the frontispiece of the MoMA catalogue. It might thus be seen as a work of some topicality. Johnson's

cast was made from the model, dating to around 1930, which had been found in Nadelman's attic, along with many other such figures, mostly on a much smaller scale. Henri Cartier-Bresson took some remarkable photographs of these serried ranks of sculpture at the house in Alderbrook. Nadelman's interest in the thickening and blurring of profiles—somewhat similar to ancient Greek Tanagras—was intensified by such basic methods of serial reproduction as the papier-mâché used here.[8] Nelson

[8] After the Wall Street Crash, Nadelman and his wife, who had lost most of her fortune, retired to their house at Alderbrook on the Hudson. There, Nadelman experimented with ceramics and papier mâché, showing none of the results, and also worked extensively in plaster.

[9] Whitney catalogue, 1975, p.90.

5.4 Elie Nadelman, *Two Circus Women*, c1930

5.5 Philip Johnson, Glass House, New Canaan, Connecticut, 1950

Rockefeller owned a bronze version of the same work[9] and of its counterpart, *Two Women*. The same figures—transposed into 19 feet of polished marble —are also in Johnson's State Theater at the Lincoln Center, which was unveiled in 1964. (Lincoln Kerstein, Nadelman's biographer, head of New York City Ballet, and friend of Nelson Rockefeller, is the link here.) The choice of the overblown, blowsy Nadelman work makes a clear contrast with the emaciated plaster Alberto Giacometti (*Night*, 1947) on the glass table.[10] Though the Nadelman has yellowed with age, the works must have shared a material impermanency and light tonal range, which might be seen as especially effective for this kind of abstract architecture.

In the extract on pages 80–81, Johnson describes a sculpture that, although inside the building, is nevertheless its foil (5.5). This wording is sufficiently unusual to be deliberate. The sculpture is at the heart of the building, but is described as its 'background'. The architectural framework is thus effectively superimposed onto the body of the sculpture. The Nadelman is very different from Kolbe's *Morning:* double not single, plump rather than stately, comic rather than dignified. It has little of Kolbe's gravity and perhaps Johnson's ludic element is in evidence here.[11] Nevertheless, *Two Circus Women* fulfils an important role, absorbing the building into itself, as it were, while at the same time throwing it off. The inversions are complex: is the figure the landscape for the house or is it the other way around? The Glass House reveals how the sculpture stands between architecture and landscape.

Whereas Mies' pavilion was a location of national representation, and his Barcelona chairs were designed for the Spanish monarchs, while his table was conceived for the *livre d'or*, Johnson's house is his own.[12] His restrained choice of works of art—the Nadelman, the small Giacometti and a Poussinesque painting—was equally carefully considered, for though he tried more contemporary paintings, he found the classical landscape most appropriate to the house's abstract quality. Here we find what the Barcelona Pavilion demonstrates: that abstract architecture is well suited to (or even requires) figuration.

Whereas Johnson seemed almost to revel in his debt to Mies in his account of his New Canaan house, the same was not the case with the MoMA garden. And though it is arguable that Johnson's understanding of landscape vistas was his own, he makes no mention in his accounts of the sculpture garden of its similarity to Mies' Museum for a Small City project. The similarities lie in the look of the collage—with its sense of transparent sliding planes, each fixed by a sculpture—in its material quality—with the screens of paving stones, water and foliage behind the sculptures—and in the sculptures themselves (5.6).

[10] The single figure sculpture on the table is not *Place*, as it is sometimes called. However, *Place* (bronze, 1950) did come into the house a little later and sat on the floor, while a small work by Mary Callery sat on the table. *Place* is the sculpture to which Johnson refers in his essay 'Whence and Whither'. *Night* was under repair by the artist at the time of his death and hence lost to Johnson. See J. Kipnis in his introduction to *Philip Johnson. The Glass House,* New York, 1993, p.16.

[11] The small guest house (1949–50) he designed for Blanchette Rockefeller in New York (after the project for her sculpture pavilion (1948) in the country was aborted) uses more 'serious' sculpture, including Giacometti's *Man Pointing* and Marini's *Rider*. (The Marini was bought from Curt Valentin, who introduced many European artists to America, especially Moore. It was here that Johnson met his companion, John Hohnsbeen, who worked there.) The long narrow Rockefeller house was divided into two parts by a small pool; a kind of semi-interior, semi-exterior court.

[12] Johnson's taste was wide-ranging and evolving. The works with which he filled his Sculpture Gallery—especially after meeting David Whitney—when it was built at New Canaan in 1970, included very recent pieces by Donald Judd, Robert Morris and Claes Oldenberg. Described by the English critic and curator Bryan Robertson as a 'rough-textured starfish', the Gallery is not unlike Rietveld's or Van Eyck's pavilions (see below) in its finish of white painted brick walls and an unpainted brick-laid floor.

[13] F. Schulze recounts that Johnson invited Mary Callery to work up a sculpture for the place between the Glass House and the Guest House, but later settled for a Lipchitz. See *Philip Johnson, Life and Work,* New York, 1994, pp.198, 235.

[14] Original lost; reproduced as the frontispiece to *Philip Johnson and the Museum of Modern Art, (Studies in Modern Art),* MoMA, ed. J. Elderfield, New York, 1998.

[15] Mies had designed the interiors of the Arts Club of Chicago at 109 East Ontario Street, which re-opened in June 1951.

5.6   Philip Johnson, The Abby Aldrich Rockefeller Sculpture Garden. View south towards the rear façade of MoMA, New York, 1953. Alexander Georges 404-1. PA238

If Johnson's architectural lineage has been well-rehearsed, the sculptural aspect has been rather less intensively pursued. And if in his own house Johnson chose Nadelman, when he worked on the MoMA garden his repertoire was much closer to that of Mies.[13] Mies' design for a Museum for a Small City (published ten years earlier) has introduced us to a type of sculpture in general and to a sculptor in particular: Maillol. In an early, unrealised plan for MoMA's sculpture garden, dated to 1948, Johnson puts Maillol's *Night*—a sculpture which had appeared in Mies' published project[14]—right in the foreground, (5.7) and in the 1953 realisation, Maillol's *River* takes centre stage. In effect, Johnson gets there first. His MoMA garden was realised before any of Mies' projects for a museum.[15]

Mies made a prolonged visit to the States in 1937, in the company of his first American client, Mrs Stanley

Resor. By 1938, he was Professor of Architecture at the Armour Institute of Technology in Chicago. Helen Resor was by then a collector,[16] who cherished Lehmbruck's work, and Lehmbruck was one of the (Miesian) artists in the collection donated by Abby Aldrich Rockefeller for which the first MoMA garden was created. Mrs Resor sat on its founding committee.[17] MoMA had dedicated an exhibition to Lehmbruck and Maillol in March 1930, showing a total of twenty-seven works, all but three of which came from American collections, private and public. By the time of the opening of the first MoMA garden in 1939, the Museum owned three key works by Lehmbruck: *Standing Female Figure* (given in 1930), *Kneeling Woman* (bought in 1939) and *Standing Youth* (donated in 1936). Just as Mies would, perhaps obsessively, use and re-use the same few sculptures within his architectural plans from this period onwards,[18] so subsequent generations of architects pick on only a very few works with which to people their spaces.

These particular sculptures add something known to an unknown space, in that they are familiar works of art. Here is another set of sculptures which has 'walked out' of the museum, bridging the unreal museum space and the reality of our own. Sculpture works on us as strongly as any painting, because it reproduces remarkably well, and better indeed than most paintings. All these sculptures have distinctive (pictorial) outlines, working as well in blueprints as in photos. *Standing Youth* was particularly loved by architects from Mies onwards, one presumes for its tense architectonic pose and recognisable profile, but perhaps also for its links to Mies. In that sense, it acts as a quick entry code for the viewer of the architectural plan, and also gives reality to something that is merely projected on paper. The reference made by these sculptures to Mies' earlier plans comes with a pedigree: they link at once to an established canon of both fine art and architecture. They are a *lingua franca*, in this sense, but what is their language? To an extent their ubiquity renders mute their individuality. Thus these sculptures read first simply as figures which one may already have seen in a number of other 'monumental' settings. Do architects use them as ready-reckoners, simply connoting the associations of the space (5.8)? Certainly the function of the sculptures goes well beyond the question of scale, if it is about scale at all. Though they often help to provide

[16] Mrs Resor had bought a Lehmbruck head from Curt Valentin in 1939. Mies' sketches of three sculptures for the Resor house are unidentified, but one suggests Lehmbruck's *Standing Female Figure* of 1910. The presentation drawing (by John Rodgers) confirms this identification and shows another unidentified, reclining, figure.

[17] Note also that between May 1939 and January 1941, the Arts Club of Chicago had dedicated exhibitions to Lehmbruck, Picasso's *Guernica*, Georges Braque, Maillol and Paul Klee; all artists used in Mies' collages.

[18] See Penelope Curtis, 'The modern eye catcher: Mies van der Rohe and sculpture', *Architectural Research Quarterly*, Cambridge, vol. 7, 3–4, 2003, pp.361–70.

[19] See Mirka Benes, 'A Modern Classic', in *Philip Johnson and the Museum of Modern Art (Studies in Modern Art 6)*, ed. J. Elderfield, New York, 1998, for a full discussion of these schemes.

[20] *Sculpture of the Twentieth Century* ran in New York from April 29 to September 7, 1953. Among 103 exhibits it included the following loans: Renoir's *Washerwoman*, Maillol's *Mediterranean*, Lehmbruck's *Seated Youth*, Jacob Epstein's *Madonna and Child*, Picasso's *Shepherd holding a Lamb* and Gerhard Marcks' *Maja*. It also showed Lachaise's *Standing Woman* and *Floating Figure*, Maillol's *River*, and Moore's *Family Group*, already in the collection.

[21] It is interesting to note that Joseph Hudnut's book on sculpture since Rodin rehearses the same repertoire, focusing especially enthusiastically on Maillol and Kolbe. He ends with a plea: 'What is wanted is a recognition by architects of their need for sculpture. Sculpture attains its greatest significance and its greatest power in the presence of an architecture that imposes its firm and lucid relationships upon it.' *Modern Sculpture*, New York, 1929, p.89.

5.7   Philip Johnson, The House of Glass, MoMA Sculpture Garden, New York, 1948

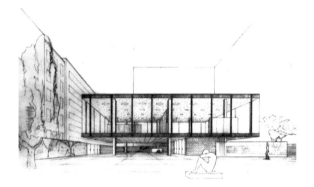

points of orientation, in terms of the way they face, their scale is not functional. Their presence and direction may help us to read a plan (and, at a later date, a building), but they seem to be as much about adding meaning as anything else.

The various plans[19] for redesigning the Museum garden between 1948 and 1952 also use and re-use a few key sculptures, including the same Lehmbruck *Standing Youth*, as well as Gaston Lachaise's *Floating Figure* (acquired 1937), and Maillol's *River* (acquired 1949) (5.9). These works had entered the collection independently, or by means of the above-mentioned exhibitions.[20] Many of the works that were shown in the new sculpture garden were only very recently acquired: Marino Marini's *Horse and Rider* in 1948, Henry Moore's *Family Group* in 1951, Henri Matisse's *Backs* in 1952 and Renoir's *Washerwoman* in 1953. This rapid coming together of a restricted group of works in outdoor space was to become a model. The American sculpture garden at mid-century was using an almost exclusively European repertoire of sculptures,[21] and represents a newly conceived canon which was to last half a century and more.

Sculptures were often used in a way that denoted leisure, or spoke of the tradition of garden statuary —*River* and *Washerwoman* denote the water that lies adjacent—but this does not fully explain why the corpus remained so restricted. It is not just that Maillol

Johnson's Fixing

22 Maillol's *River* was one of about sixteen sculptures to be placed in the new 'Musée Maillol', created in the Gardens of the Carrousel between the Louvre and the Tuileries in 1964–5. This act, presented as the first open-air museum, was a collaborative gesture on the part of artist's companion Dina Vierny (who offered the artist's original models), and André Malraux (French Minister of Cultural Affairs 1959–69), who arranged for the State's ateliers to have them cast. Maillol had already been represented by two sculptures—the *Monument à Cézanne* and *Mediterranée*—in the Tuileries gardens from the late 1920s through to the early 1960s, when they were withdrawn in order to preserve their stone.

23 Elizabeth B. Mock was Acting Director of the Department of Architecture from 1942/3 to 1946. Her 1964 book was published under her married name of Kassler.

24 The designs of Skidmore, Owings and Merrill predominate, alongside those of Barragan, Burle Marx, and a number of contemporary Scandinavians.

5.8 'Lehmbruck Gallery', MoMA, New York, 1954

in the first instance, and then Marini, Matisse and Moore should feature again and again, but that particular works by them can be repeatedly found in the outdoor collections built up in the post-war period.[22] Sculpture's silhouettes and profiles enter our minds, and we have the opportunity of re-encountering them, in different places and in different contexts, because of their reproduceability. This is a major part of sculpture's fascination. Sculpture is a reproductive art, and collectors took advantage of this. They wanted the same, rather than different, and they iterated other gardens, at home or abroad. The endlessly repeated actions of the sculptures are thus repeated across space as well as time.

The recently completed MoMA sculpture garden features among the choice examples illustrated by Johnson's MoMA colleague Elizabeth Mock in her 1964 book *Modern Gardens and the Landscape*.[23] It is included in a sequence of photos which shows how the constructed garden (the paved garden or *jardin dallé*) had emerged out of the flat modernist 'painterly' garden compositions of the late 1920s, through an interest in Japanese gardens, into some of the Californian decked and paved courts, in which a luxuriant nature is controlled and kept at bay.[24] Along with many of the MoMA garden's first reviewers, Mock calls this phenomenon the 'outdoor room'. The illustrations and text suggest that hard architecture —walls and paving—based on a grid plan can provide a pleasing enclosure by means of its delimiting capability. Mock suggests that the American convention of leaving houses 'open' to the landscape had in fact led to the popularity of hidden spaces (or courts) within their walls, providing their inhabitants with more secluded access to the open air. Mock's presentation shows how Johnson's sculpture garden takes its place within the context of European and American 'gardens' which are built rather than grown, and which are extensions of the buildings rather than of the grounds around them.

Johnson's design reveals a wider shift in thinking about the garden which, in his case, reflects his recent period at Harvard, where Joseph Hudnut had become Dean in 1935. Hudnut had integrated the design departments and promoted a cohesive understanding and indeed a more fulsome embrace of the garden as an important component of modernist architecture. Although responsible for modernising the school, Hudnut later fell out with Gropius, whose appointment he had secured in 1937. In 1939, Hudnut invited Christopher Tunnard—who is best known to English readers for his use of a Henry Moore sculpture on the terrace of Bentley Wood in Sussex—to teach at Harvard, where he made a point of emphasising the suitability of modern sculpture to the landscape. Tunnard stayed only three years, but had a significant impact.[25]

The 1953 MoMA sculpture garden drew largely from a recent tradition of architecture (principally of houses) rather than from a longer tradition of gardens.[26] The pavilion model is thus merged with that of the patio. It is clear that the plan resembles Mies' court houses as much as anything, and the key shift is perhaps not simply that here Johnson has taken the room outdoors, as he said, but that he has made a garden out of a house. The pools are less about water as such, and more about replicating the blank oblong spaces—the screens and rugs—of the modernist interior. Such rectilinear spaces both support and penetrate the sculpture and the furniture which is laid over them, just as Mies' drawn grids support their collaged additions.

But if it is domestic in origin, the Museum garden must also be seen as public in intent. It lies within the post-war concern for a humanised city centre, and thus we can understand the conjunction of figurative sculpture with the 'greening' of the urban space. This coincides with the discussions on the new monumentality that were touched upon in the last chapter, and with which Johnson was also concerned. As early as September 1945, in an article in *Art News*, he extolled the monuments of the past, from the mound to the megalith, but lamented the monumental art of the last hundred years. He attributed the fault to functionalism, which had no relevance to the design of monuments.[27]

Johnson's article was written in the context of the war memorial, but he seemed disappointed by Hudnut's plea that 'we build playgrounds, schoolhouses, parks, anything rather than "to increase the dreadful population" of our monuments'.[28] Johnson did not relish the 'large crop of useful, or what are called "living" memorials [which we may expect] after this war'.

[25] This was Johnson's second stint there. After travelling and working with Alfred Barr and Henry-Russell Hitchcock, he returned to Harvard in autumn 1940 and was there until Spring 1943, when he was drafted into the army. Three other students who were to become notable landscape architects—Garrett Eckbo, Dan Kiley and James Rose—had also arrived at Harvard in the late 1930s, and it was apparently they who persuaded Hudnut to invite Tunnard. Johnson was certainly one of Tunnard's students. See L.M. Neckar, 'Christopher Tunnard's *Gardens in the Modern Landscape*', *Journal of Garden History*, vol.10, no. 4, 1990, pp.241–2.

[26] Some of the sculpture parks that were to open in the 1960s—Storm King and the Kröller-Müller at Otterlo—used a much more open and extensive canvas, and, in their scale and form, allowed for the introduction of newer American abstract sculpture. The city centre gardens, however, as seen in MoMA, and then in the Tuileries (1964–5), UCLA (1967), at the Hirshorn (1974), and even the Nasher (2003), remained faithful to a much more introverted figurative repertory.

[27] 'War Memorials: What Aesthetic Price Glory?', *Art News*, September 1945, quoted by F. Schulze in *Philip Johnson, Life and Work*, New York, 1994, pp.174–5.

[28] Ibid., p.9.

[29] Ibid., p.25.

5.9 Philip Johnson, The Abby Aldrich Rockefeller Sculpture Garden. East view, MoMA, New York, 1953. Photographed 1953 by Alexander Georges PA485

Arguing against the utilitarian approach, he neverthe-less admitted that it was unlikely that the nation's committees would commission a commemorative work of the quality of *Guernica*. More realistically, he puts forward alternative categories, such as tablets, fountains, exedrae and flagpoles, which could be used imaginatively, but also a few exceptional sculptors: Barlach, Lehmbruck, Maillol, Lipchitz and Moore.[29] Ironically enough, it is arguable that within six years, Johnson had himself created what he had earlier den-igrated as a 'living memorial' in the shape of the MoMA sculpture garden. For as he became increasingly interested in the concept of monumentality, show-ing it in his own architecture with heavier and more overtly historicising arches and colonnades, might we not also see the MoMA sculpture garden as both a new monumental space (for the communal life of

the city), and as an old monumental space, in the sense of an artistic memorial? Johnson's garden was at once a space that, like other memorial parks and playgrounds, marked the end of war with a commitment to the future, but also, through its inclusion of a certain range of artwork, looked back to an earlier kind of figurative memorial indicating loss.

Why the architect uses sculpture is not the question here; it was, after all, the purpose of the commission. Johnson is effectively working with an exisiting collection (even if the garden opened with an exhibition). He had no part in commissioning any sculpture, or indeed, according to his later interviews, in placing it, which was done by Alfred Barr. Nevertheless, what the sculptures give the architecture, and what his architecture gives them, is worth unpicking.

Johnson has made a park, or a museum, but he has

[30] These sculptures had not been designed for the 'sculpture park' as such. The evolution of this new kind of space—which emerged out of the post-war exhibitions of outdoor sculpture shown in the London parks, and at Arnhem's Sonsbeek, which were themselves closely associated with war-time destruction and recovery—saw the development of a new category of sculpture specifically designed for the landscape.

5.10 Philip Johnson, The Abby Aldrich Rockefeller Sculpture Garden, MoMA, New York, 1953

also made a space which has its own gravitas (5.10).[30] In this space, he uses an existing repertoire of European figurative sculpture, shaped by war and by the commemorative traditions of figurative sculpture. These sculptures may not have been overtly representative of those whom they commemorated, but they are levers which act to bring us into that space, for they either look as if they are markers of something beyond themselves, or are known to have been used in that way. His garden contributes to the provision of shared experience, and it does this not only through the architecture, but also (and perhaps more so) by means of the sculptures.

The works are only semi-human. Even those that are most ordinary, like Gerhard Marcks' *Maya* or Renoir's *Washerwoman*, are rendered strange by the unchanging continuity of their activity. They are strange because they make their own spaces, which are unaffected by the viewer, who may be able to 'read' their activity, and even imagine that action, but who has no experience of it as such. These sculptures are not figurative in any simple way. They do not do what we do. Even the simplest actions are rendered strange by their unchangingness. They thus exist in a space which is at once attainable and unattainable. The statues are moreover deeply self-absorbed. The 'activity' of Lehmbruck is as much mental as physical, sometimes almost trance-like, and its formal self-containment draws us in. The other works do something similar, if in a less attenuated way: Renoir's washerwoman endlessly holds up her laundry; Lachaise's figure keeps her balance by dint of self-will; Maillol's *River* is poised between being pulled into her element and retaining her form as sculpture on the edge of the pool (5.11).

Formally, the sculptures give their unfixed environment relatively small punctuation points of great density. In a largely homogenous bronze, they are placed as if strung out on the invisible scaffolding of the architecture. They mark its uprights and verticals, and they pin it to the ground. They can hardly be said to 'people' the space, for the effect of these sculptures is not quotidian. Their formal effect is therefore architectural rather than human. The sculptures do not represent the human being; they represent the architecture. Their narrative effect adds something to the architecture, but something which is less about

Johnson's Fixing

31 It was Hudnut who had invited Giedion to give the Norton lectures at Harvard in 1938–9, which then became the famous book *Space, Time and Architecture*.

5.11   Aristide Maillol, *The River* (begun 1938–39, completed 1943), MoMA, New York

mimetic human experience and more about the abstract qualities of space and time.[31] The sculptured actions are thus given significance, although they have no significance as such. Space and time confer importance. Trivial actions become timeless. There are sufficient pointers—the sober and collected human aspect, the material, the positioning—to tell us that these works have meaning, although their actions are in fact meaningless. Their 'movement' is not movement, and this is what is so strange in this space, for it is like a film still, in which everything—in its ultimately unimportant 'business'—has suddenly been stopped.

SCARPA'S ILLUMINATION: THE GIPSOTECA CANOVIANA (1957)

In Possagno, north of Venice and Treviso, is the collection of plaster casts left to his birthplace by the sculptor Antonio Canova (1757–1822). The self-proclaiming Gypsotheca, Museo Canoviano was housed in an imposing, purpose-built basilica-type building erected in the early 1830s. In 1955, the architect Carlo Scarpa (1906–78) was invited to extend this building for the 200th anniversary of Canova's birth. Though Scarpa's 'extension' is a great deal smaller than the original Gipsoteca, and inserts itself into an irregularly-shaped and almost ignominious fillet of land down one side of the basilica, it has consistently excited great enthusiasm.

By 1955, Scarpa had garnered experience with a range of installation projects, and had recently begun working on the museum renovations with which he made his name. His early career in the Murano glassworks meant that as early as 1927, Scarpa was involved in the presentation of objects at exhibitions and in showrooms. From 1933 to 1947 he designed the booths for Venini, and he was represented in this way at both the VI and the VII Milan Triennales. In these displays, he was arranging objects in relation to one another, and he would incorporate some of the vocabulary allowed to retail display—notably screens and curtains—into his museum work.

Scarpa's work in the field of tomb architecture, which began in the early 1940s, must have been equally influential on his thinking about the presentation of the single object in space. His screen-like presentation of information and imagery in the museum invariably starts with the single upright form, as exemplified in the restoration work he embarked upon in 1953 at the Palazzo Abatellis in Palermo. Here, as in a number of his installations, Scarpa puts paintings on screens and brings them off the wall, specifying the joints of their supports and frames in the most careful detail. The Italian word for fitting-out—*allestimento*—which is also used for 'installation', carries with it the echoes of other Italian 'trade' terms which help us to understand Scarpa's method of working.

Scarpa's close friendship with the sculptor Arturo Martini may have helped establish his use of pieces of stilled figuration, each with a clear and recognisable profile. Living and working in the same region,

Scarpa even lodged with Martini for a year in 1940, decorated his apartment in 1941, and designed his Venice Biennale presentation in 1942. Martini had been one of the most effective providers of statues during the 1920s and 1930s, never affiliating himself to, nor distancing himself from, the Fascist regime, but regularly producing striking monumental statuary of mystery and distinction. His works show single or double figures, in stone or bronze, largely locked into their own worlds and excluding us from their space.

Scarpa was deeply influenced by contemporary art beyond the work of Martini. Many argue that his installation of the work of Paul Klee for the Venice Biennale of 1948 was the single most important encounter and influence for his understanding of space.[1] From then on, Scarpa was intimately associated with the Venice Biennale, designing two independent pavilions and many different temporary presentations. In 1952, he designed the sculpture courtyard for the Italian Pavilion, which was 'furnished' with the work of contemporary sculptor Alberto Viani, but the bulk of his museum career was concerned with historic buildings and artworks.

In a later lecture to his students,[2] Scarpa gave some interesting details about the Possagno commission, which are rarely remarked upon in the secondary literature. He posited that the initial imperative came from the imminent arrival from the Accademia in Venice of a large plaster which required a new high space. Scarpa seems to have seen this as a political rather than an actual necessity, but nevertheless got to work on the brief. Unsure of the work in question—but remembering it as a 'Theseus or something of the sort'—he came to realise how boring it would be to put a high object in a high room.[3] Having convinced the scholars of this, he then had the chance to choose his own sculptures according to the composition that he desired: 'So instead we pick out certain important sculptures from among those exhibited here—rather badly—to arrange them according to an instinctive sense of the arrangement of particular elements, which must be the most important thing in a museum.'[4]

The choice in the Scarpa wing of the sculptures themselves is rarely discussed, but is in fact subtly different from that in the main Basilica.[5] Where those

[1] Mies van der Rohe, Scarpa and Aldo van Eyck all loved the work of Klee.

[2] 'Volevo ritagliare l'azzurro del cielo', 13 January 1976, reprinted in Quaderns d'arquitectura i urbanisme 158, August/Sept 1983, pp.21–4. All subsequent quotations from Scarpa come from this article; translation is my own. Another version, with similar and different passages, is given in French by Françoise Brun in Les cahiers de la recherche architecturale, no. 19, 1986, pp.94–103.

[3] This would seem to be Teseo in Lotta con il Centauro, the marble of which is in Vienna, and which, prior to its arrival in Possagno 'in tempi recenti', was in the Accademia di Venezia. It measures 340 x 372 x 152cm. G. Pavanello, L'Opera completa del Canova. Milan, 1976, p.113. Scarpa's story is corroborated by Paola Marini in the Verona/Vicenza catalogue of 2000, Carlo Scarpa, Milan, 2000, p.136. She adds that another key concern was to have the bozzetti properly housed.

[4] 'Togliamo invece alcune statue importante fra quelle disposte qui—fra l'altro male—per disporle secondo il senso dell'intuizione compositiva di certi elementi che devono essere la cosa piu importante per un museo.'

[5] It seems that Scarpa also slightly re-arranged the Basilica, placing the Hercules group in the apse where Religion had previously been. Christine Hoh-Slodczyk, Carlo Scarpa und das Museum, Berlin, 1987, p.16.

6.1   Carlo Scarpa, Gipsoteca Canoviana, Possagno

pieces tend to be more formal—to be upright, to be commemorative, and to include more men—the sculptures in the new wing are largely female, ideal works, and many are recumbent (6.1). Scarpa's lecture makes it clear how it was this aspect of Canova which most appealed to him. (This was not the first time he had dealt with Canova: his 1949 plans for remodelling the Accademia Galleries in Venice had included a gallery for Canova's sculptures.) Unlike the Basilica, which feels a great deal more masculine and remote, if not somewhat pompous, Scarpa gives his small spaces, and the sculptures which they contain, an intimacy which is both informal and dignified.

Scarpa's wing—which is almost literally a wing in its L-shaped form—provides three spaces. The threshold between the old space and the new is marked first by a complicated double/triple step,

Scarpa's Illumination

and then by the 'removal' of a section of the skirting board that would otherwise appear to bind the room as if it were a shallow pool (6.2). The first, atrium-like, space leads onto both the high gallery and onto a long triangular gallery, which are at right-angles to each other. This latter space would seem at first to flow smoothly down to its apex (6.3). A small, dark skirting board in black metal threads down the levels and into the pool outside. Despite this fluidity, there are in fact three sections to this long gallery, and the space as a whole is made to seem larger and more complex by the play of levels and divisions. Two double steps take you down rather steeply from the first level to the next, and the final two sections are divided by a tiny vestigial step. These breaks and continuities are unfamiliar and make one experience a trepidation similar to that of Scarpa's later Querini Stampalia in Venice.[6] These are not spaces in which to relax, but in which to be aware—even if the sculptures themselves sleep peacefully—and if Baudelaire and countless others said that sculpture is something you bump into, here it is the architecture which is more likely to trip you up.

The arrangement of the marble floor tiles plays its part in differentiating in an almost sub-conscious fashion the spaces which the viewer will experience. Whereas the high gallery is regularly tiled, its atrium and the first of the three levels of the long gallery are laid with larger, slightly irregular tiles. The last gallery, in which stands the *Three Graces*, is tiled in much smaller sections, and in a less rectilinear manner. The different levels of the floor are echoed in the ceiling, and with greater emphasis. Four high, almost castellated semi-opaque windows turn back on themselves at a right angle which echoes the shape of the 'pavilion' windows framing the *Three Graces*.[7] The light appears to be largely behind the sculpture—or in nature—although one later sees how the pavilion's fenestration wraps around and back into the building. The whole is like a series of inter-locking L-shapes.

Whereas the Basilica is arranged symmetrically, the Scarpa wing pulls the works out and alternates them with each other, like a series of irregular planes that nevertheless make up a whole. The circuit—which can be emphasised by the sculpture—is not direct, but zig-zagged, inter-locutional, phased. In the long

[6] And also to an extent at Trieste's Museo Revoltella 1963/67, incomplete.

[7] This fenestration can be compared to that in his Venezuelan pavilion for the Venice Biennale, 1954–6.

6.2 (previous pages) Carlo Scarpa, Museo Canoviano, Possagno, view of the entrance

6.3 Carlo Scarpa, Gipsoteca Canoviana, Possagno

gallery, the vitrines, with their pairs of bozzetti, break the view and need to be looked into rather than at. During this section of the parcours, close-focus is the means of looking, and thus one's progress is effectively staggered before arriving at the final sculpture, the *Three Graces*, which is itself set off-centre. The encounter with this most famous group is thus delayed, and only after one has descended the levels, and got past the vitrines, is one able to gain a satisfactory viewing position. In this respect then, the *Three Graces* seems both to be placed in the tradition of terminal sculpture (and there is an example right next door, in the original Basilica of the Canoviana, with the *Hercules* group[8] occupying the apse) and to break with it.

The long gallery inserts itself, like a wedge, into the countryside on the edge of the town. The light-weight, seemingly provisional nature of its final aperture is unusual for Scarpa, whose work is generally integrated into its context by means of the materiality of the surrounding fabric. For if we see Mies' Concert Hall or Museum for a Small City as leading to the open warehouse type of fluid and changing museum installation, Scarpa exemplifies the 'Italian School' approach, developed during the same years, in which specific pieces of art dictate specific conditions for their permanent installation. The Italian situation created the conditions for *réaménagement*, in which a country replete with historical works of art and with historical buildings redefines this heritage (which may have been additionally damaged by war) by means of careful realignment in order to bring it into the modern world.

Though it is something of a commonplace[9] that the post-war Italian School was a deliberate reaction to a Fascist aesthetic, is this really sustainable? One might argue that Scarpa's installational skills derived from the very emphasis placed on exhibition design during the Fascist period. Scarpa himself was involved as a designer at the 1936 Milan Triennale, which, as we have seen, used sculpture in surprisingly innovative but nonetheless 'significant' (or monumental) ways. The methods, and the terminology that can be used to define his work — *isolazione, valorizzazione* — are reminiscent of the Fascist era and in particular of the wholesale scenographic efforts to valorise the significant monuments of Imperial

[8] *Ercole e Saetta i figli*, 335 x 220 x 130 cm, also deposited at Possagno by the Accademia di Venezia 'in tempi recenti'. See Pavanello, op. cit., p.107.

[9] Richard Murphy, *Carlo Scarpa and the Castelvecchio*, London, 1990, p.18.

[10] Albini at the Palazzo Bianco (1950–1) and the Treasury (1956), both in Genoa; BBPR at Castello Sforzesco, Milan (1954–64).

Rome. An installation technique that mounted solid nuggets (or fragments) of historical or factual matter against open architectonic frameworks, as exemplified in much of the work of Albini, BBPR, Gardella or of Persico, reverberates in the post-war years, notably in the work of Scarpa.[10]

While it is indisputable that Italian conditions produced a certain kind of museum project, it may be wrong to separate the Scarpa museum project too completely from that of Mies. On the contrary, we can see much that they have in common, and not least their interest in the screens and frames which hold paintings, mid-air, off the wall. Scarpa's methodology also allows sculptures to be placed in relation to one another without overlapping, and the Miesian collage is an effective parallel here. Each profile works in relation to the next, for the silhouette is important to both Mies and Scarpa. Profiles echo and complement profiles. Scarpa's high gallery, especially, provides an image which is extremely effective in two-dimensions, with one profile fitting into another, shadowing but countering the surrounding silhouettes, while the works are individually differentiated by the varying degrees of light which fall on them according to their range (their closeness to or distance from the viewer) (6.4). One clear difference between Mies and Scarpa is in the way in which they present their sculptures: Scarpa lifts them off the ground, whereas Mies only does this with paintings. Scarpa designs their plinths; Mies simply puts them on the ground. Mies is largely working with images; Scarpa only with the real thing.

Scarpa's plinths themselves vary notably in their make-up. Some—*Eros & Psyche*—are cut precisely to the contours of the sculpture, others—*Monument to George Washington*—are split vertically and horizontally, as if they were blocks brought together to make a whole. Others are like low daybeds—see *Sleeping Nymph*—in which a bed of stone and concrete is supported on a low iron table. Smaller pieces are 'thrown' into the air, either higher up, on small shelves, or in the glass vitrines, which stand on welded iron legs. The sculptures—such as *Bust of Napoleon*—on iron shelves which pierce the wall directly seem to be mirrored by the windows above them, which are inserted into the space as

if they too were resting on their support. The vitrines also echo the window casements in their design, and are thus enhanced in their somewhat otherworldly feel.

Scarpa provides us with more views than did Mies, and with more times of day. The idea of drawing with light, as if in grisaille, is emphasised by the fact that the walls are white, just like the plasters. Scarpa matches surfaces and treatments. There was doubt about his colour-scheme (which is hardly a 'colour-scheme' at all, in the conventional sense), but his careful consideration paid off, and he convinced his peers, partly by arguing against the north light, which he saw as one of the causes of dislike of 'cold' neo-classical works such as Canova's. He was

6.4   Carlo Scarpa, Gipsoteca Canoviana, Possagno

6.5   Carlo Scarpa, Gipsoteca Canoviana, Possagno

well aware of the special need for light, especially given the predominance of plaster. Being plasters, they were, in Scarpa's words *amorfo*, needing their 'place in the sun' (*un posto al sole*) (6.5). In the first, high gallery, the foliage and the sky are dreamlike, caught in the four windows and framed by them. But the windows are also demonstrative: they show the sky—and its light—rather than hiding it.

The plaster of both the walls and of the works, and the fact that the sculptures are full of pointing holes (measurements for copying the marble version), picks up on this architect's tendency to cut into his own surfaces, and to insert dark metal into their tender white walls. There is a similar interventionist quality in the penetrations into the body of the building or

Scarpa's Illumination

[11] 'Questi punti neri sui corpi giovani di donne nude sono di un fascino indescrivible.'

[12] 'Guardate come dorme tranquilla quella signora! Vedete che braccio e che dorso? Sono straordinario! Non vi dico dei glutei visti dal di sopra!'

[13] 'Quella testa e invece antipatica: viene proprio voglia di romparla.'

[14] The group reached England in May 1819 and was installed that summer at Woburn Abbey. Hugh Honour, 'Canova's Three Graces', in *The Three Graces*, Edinburgh, 1995, p.43. The transition from greenhouse into sculpture gallery proper at Woburn was established gradually, but above all after Canova's visit in 1815. The Duke's architect joined the party, and produced plans for the Temple of the Graces, to be inserted at one end of the long conservatory/gallery, soon after.

[15] See John Kenworthy-Browne on 'The Sculpture Gallery' in the above volume, pp.61–71.

6.6   Antonio Canova, *The Three Graces*, 1813–1816, Gipsoteca Canoviana, Possagno

the body of the sculpture. The pointing measurements have a quite extraordinary effect on the sculptures, at once emphasising and dematerialising their materiality, like a transparent veil laid over a solid work of art (6.6). Scarpa himself noted that the black marks on the 'young bodies of naked woman were indescribably fascinating'.[11]

Scarpa defended Canova from charges of a neoclassical coldness by countering with Canova's extraordinary formal comprehension of the female statue: 'See how that woman sleeps peacefully. Do you see her arms and her back! They are extraordinary. I can't tell you about the buttocks seen from above!'[12] He admires the body if not the head: 'The head on the other hand is dislikeable; it makes you want to break it.'[13] He works with the body, and with our sensual response to the body. Scarpa's Canoviana—so to speak—is feminine.

The *Three Graces* had been commissioned, and the subject suggested, by the Empress Josephine. The Possagno plaster (1813) is the model for her piece, now in the Hermitage. Another version was commissioned by the Duke of Bedford for his ancestral seat in Woburn Abbey. Canova had himself inspected the site at Woburn, and after his visit, work began there on the construction of the Temple of the Graces within the existing gallery.[14] The presentation of the *Three Graces*—in a circular temple at one end of a converted conservatory—sets up an interesting dialogue with Scarpa's at Possagno. (A parallel example is the *Hercules*, also at the end of the adjoining Basilica, which represents the other piece that Canova had himself helped to place, in the rotunda at the end of the Palazzo Torlonia.) The Woburn Temple—which had a diameter of c. 4.5 metres and was lit from above by an oculus c. 1.5 metres in diameter—was approached through a semi-circular space of similar diameter, and the sculpture was framed by an oblong doorway with steps up to the level on which the sculpture, lifted high on an 'antique' plinth, was displayed. Whereas the spaces above and below it were richly decorated, the wall against which the sculpture was read was in a plain yellow scagliola.[15]

Scarpa also puts this feminine sculpture in a protected position, lit from above as well as from the back (6.7). And again it is in a garden situation, made more overt in Possagno with its backdrop of pool and greenery.[16] The sculpture is thus given space in which to expand, and with it we too are extended an invitation to reverie. Scarpa manifestly designed with certain sculptures, or certain types of sculptures, in mind. His discussion of the lighting of the *Three Graces* shows how specifically it was positioned, and illuminated:

> I wanted to place the *Three Graces* of Canova, and thus I was thinking of a very high window: I pulled it inwards because I wanted to obtain the effect of the light being squared. This backwards return, this dihedron that enters the room allows for a quality of light that is so fine that it renders it as luminous as the other walls.[17]

Although Scarpa is working with a permanent collection, and though his building is also permanent, by the time we arrive at the *Three Graces*, we sense the fundamentally temporary nature of the 'pavilion' in

[16] Scarpa apparently greatly admired the famous triangular garden designed by Gabriel Guevrekian for the Vicomte de Noailles on the Côte d'Azur. B. Albertini and S. Bagnoli, *Scarpa: Musei ed Esposizioni,* Milan, 1992, p.31.

[17] 'volevo collocare le "Tre Grazie" del Canova, e quindi pensavo ad una vetrata molto alta: l'ho tirata verso l'interno perche volevo ottenere un effetto di luce di riquadro. Quel ritorno indietro, quel diedro che entra dentro la stanza permette quella finezza di luce in quel punto che lo rende luminoso quanto le altre pareti.'

[18] Milk of lime (*grassello*) is applied in layers with a trowel or spatula onto a base of smooth plaster (*calce*) to achieve a smooth, shiny surface.

6.7   Carlo Scarpa, Gipsoteca Canoviana, Possagno

its original sense. The four long vertical panels of glass are divided only within the fenestration, without being framed at its edges, thus giving the impression of openness, as if the funnel-shape will lead us directly to the pool. The sculpture's reflection against the foliage behind mirrors that of Kolbe's *Morning*, and it is lifted to the requisite height by a small concrete plinth (which mirrors its own footprint) to allow it to do this. The polished floor and ceiling (like the walls, in *grassello di calce*, applied with a spatula)[18] also mirror the foliage. Standing outside, where the glass is apparently uncurtailed across its horizontal limit, we feel even more strongly that this is a porous garden space. Looking backwards, in this way, we see the hills behind, rising steeply, as if we were caught by them in this pool enclosure with the sculpture (6.8).

It is clear that Scarpa did not simply design a new wing for the museum curators to use as they wished. The sculptures are part of his design, which would lose sense without them, or if they were differently configured. This fixity is important. The wall-mounted shelves are obviously indelibly fixed, but the pieces on the floor are in fact equally permanent. A drawing[19] and a plan show his careful delineation of the plinths, and the shift from the plan to the realisation. Both reveal the diamond-like positioning (point to the wall) of the pedestal vitrines on the east side of the wing, but in the final arrangement, the *Three Graces* is additionally pulled out and off the rectilinear, as are the vitrines along the west wall. The overall effect is to knock the axis onto the diagonal, but also to effect a clearer passageway and vista towards the Graces themselves.

If we were to choose the 'key' destination point of the museum's circulation, we would almost certainly choose the *Three Graces*. Why? Because they are furthest away from the door, because they are backed by foliage, and because they seem almost to hover above the pool outside. In all these aspects, we might compare them to the pavilion with which we started—Barcelona—and indeed here we are placed somewhere between conservatory and pavilion.[20] In each, we are caught with the naked female body at the furthest point from the door, against a background of nature, in a space which, with its views of outside, promises but denies egress. Instead, we are invited to spend time with the sculpture, led to it and enclosed with it in a lower, more intimate space, and then to retrace our steps through the building that we traversed too quickly to get here.

Scarpa is known for his knowledge of and interest in using old materials, traditional techniques and existing pieces of architecture, but can we extend the analogy to his use of historic sculpture? He is known for his way of joining old and new, as he did with the buildings at Possagno, but how do we bring the sculpture into this discussion? Can sculpture work as a subject and also function as a technical device?

Scarpa's most celebrated museum transformation is that in Verona, at the Castelvecchio. Here, the positioning of the historic equestrian statue of Cangrande[21] is both pivot and lock; it is mobile and static, or about mobility and about stasis. Its positioning was studied extensively by Scarpa from 1961

[19] Reproduced in *Quaderns*, as at note 2, p.13.

[20] See *metron*, 38, October 1950, for an enthusiastic response to Scarpa's 'padiglione del libro', which was admired for its anti-monumental character: 'E' un fulmine a ciel sereno o...uno spacco di sereno tra le tempestose tenebre della follia monumentale' (p.19).

[21] The Cangrande statue depicts a member of the Della Scala family, Lord of Verona 1311–29. It was once one of three statues placed on high columns in the Piazza dei Signori, and then high up on Sta Maria Antica. It had thus always been seen from below. Ruskin drew the statue—showing it set above the Scala sarcophagus—and was fascinated by the Count's smile. This information is drawn from R. Murphy, op. cit., p.111.

[22] Another interesting example is Scarpa's use of Donatello in the 'Poesia' section of the Italian pavilion at the Montreal *Expo '67*. *Athys* (Little Eros) greeted the visitor on entering the pavilion, and down below a 'perfect copy' of *David* was isolated on a large, raised patio. This floor was itself remarkable, for even if one did not know that it derived from another illustrious Italian artwork (Piero's *Flagellation*) it would strike the eye as being out of scale, enormously enlarged against the sculpture. *David* waits, alone, on the floor of the empty hall.

6.8   Carlo Scarpa, Gipsoteca Canoviana, Possagno

before its final placement in 1964 (6.9). This sculpture gives human body to the bewildering array of shapes and textures of the space around it. The statue is afforded an apparently impossible and yet entirely believable position on a concrete platform, raised up high in the centre of the building, and is viewable in different ways, from different angles, and from different kinds of material supports. The statue thus provides the concentration which synthesises the space around it. In offering itself in the traditional role of 'focal point' it in fact serves to make sense of the multiple spatial experiences by which it is surrounded.

A single sculpture can articulate the space around it in a way that a painting can never do.[22] (This may well be why Scarpa worked at making paintings sculptural.) A sculpture can be seen from different sides, but also from above and below (as with Cangrande), and from outside and in. Cangrande is interestingly both inside and outside, still a part of its native city, breathing in its air, and yet within the museum. A sculpture can be discovered once and then again, at different points of a journey round the building. This kind of inhabitation of space seems to embody the best of the Italian tradition as a *paese d'arte,* in which art is a part of the atmosphere of everyday life. Cangrande della Scala represents the city's past in the person of one of its most significant historical figures, represented in a form that conflates emblem and effigy.

Sculpture is constantly pulled back to the monument, back to the tomb. In the case of the Canoviano, the analogy is even more severe. Scarpa is working in the hometown of the sculptor. A few hundred metres away is the temple, the Tempio Canoviano, that Canova had designed and which was to become his place of burial. Next door is the Gypsotheca Museo Canoviano, a basilica-shaped space, full of tomb sculpture. By contrast the *Three Graces* is made by Scarpa to look at home in the museum but equally comfortable in the space of the pavilion, which 'lets' it into the world outside.[23] The scale of the Scarpa extension is closer to that of the outbuildings—to Canova's workshops—than to that of the original museum. By giving his sculptures a temporary feel, as if they were waiting to be carved, and only then to be released into the real world, at an undisclosed and future moment, Scarpa makes the plasters seem alive rather than dead, or about becoming rather than about recording.

What does Scarpa need to do with what is, in this case, almost literally a mausoleum? He needs to give it life. This is what his architecture gives Canova's sculpture. He puts it on the threshold, between indoors and outdoors, between past and future, between life and death.

[23] The Kolbe, on the other hand, like the Barcelona Pavilion itself, was very much in borrowed space, temporarily ceded to the German government by the city of Barcelona.

6.9   Castelvecchio Museum, Verona, with a view of 'Cangrande'

SONSBEEK'S QUESTION: PAVILIONS BY RIETVELD AND VAN EYCK (1955–66)

[1] *Sonsbeek '55, Internationale Beeldententoonstelling in de open lucht*, 28 May–15 September 1955.

[2] The host nation presented twenty artists, largely through small works or with single contributions. There were thirty-one French artists, nineteen Italian, five Swiss, four British, three from Belgium, Spain and Germany, two from the USA and one from Austria (my reckoning, using the catalogue of the exhibition). The more recent French contribution—Giacometti, Picasso and Richier—is represented only sparsely, as is the younger generation of British artists: Reg Butler, Kenneth Armitage and F.E. McWilliam.

The 1955 international open-air sculpture exhibition held in the Sonsbeek Park in Arnhem was the third of a series. The Sonsbeek exhibitions were initiated in 1949, and the second was held in 1952. In *Sonsbeek '55*[1] nearly 200 sculptures were on show. Works by living sculptors were mixed with historical works by Barlach, Bernard, Bourdelle, Degas, Duchamp-Villon, González, Lehmbruck, Maillol, Rodin, Rosso and Wlérick. Rodin had seven works, including the full-sized *Walking Man* and *Balzac;* Bourdelle had six, including *Penelope* and *Heracles*. Of any artist, alive or dead, Lehmbruck was easily the best represented, with fifteen works, including his *Thinker, Standing Youth* and *Fallen*.

Without explicitly referring to the recent division of Europe, this selection has a tale to tell. The combination of historical figures with contemporary ones stressed a figurative tradition embodied primarily in the French school. Lehmbruck apart (and he might be seen to have a particular and anomalous position), we begin with Rodin, move into Bourdelle and Maillol, continue with Laurens and Lipchitz, and with the French classicists of the inter-war years: Bernard, Despiau, Gimond, Wlérick, Pompon. Though many were recently deceased, the selection seems to use these artists to affirm a continuity in figurative sculpture now taken up by artists in England (in the shape of Moore), and above all in Italy.[2]

The many German artists who had worked—for better or for worse—in the figurative tradition in the same period—are clearly excluded. The only German artists who are included are those who died before the Third Reich began. There is thus an unspoken bias at the heart of this exhibition that promotes the viability (and the nationality) of the figurative tradition after World War II. A visitor to Arnhem in 1955 would have seen bodies and heads: small bodies in vitrines, larger ones on low socles, and heads on plinths. Although it is strikingly an exhibition of figurative and not of abstract sculpture (no Brancusi, no Hepworth), it is even more strikingly an edited version of the recent figurative tradition, from which an artist such as Kolbe was excluded.

In addition to being historical, the selection would certainly seem to have aimed at being contemporary, partly by including notably topical pieces such as Reg Butler's winning maquette for the 1952 'Unknown Political Prisoner Competition',[3] a version of Moore's *Time Life Screen*, and Germaine Richier's *Devil*. Significant works about the war would also seem to have been selected, including González's *Montserrat Head*, Zadkine's *Prisoner*, and the Butler. Moore's *Warrior* was at the heart of the installation, and Moore is seen to be the artist who has emerged, post-war, to occupy the position in which we have seen Lehmbruck and Maillol hitherto. Moore was represented at *Sonsbeek '55* with six works, including important ones like *Draped Reclining Figure*, *Reclining Figure* and the *Warrior with Shield*.

Sonsbeek was an 'open air' exhibition that derived a good deal of its impetus from the series begun in Battersea Park by the London County Council in 1948. This series, conceived by a left-wing municipality in the spirit of war-time reconstruction and of a new cultural democracy, was always shown entirely outdoors, in various city-centre London parks. Being outdoors was the key signifier of the show's aspiration: to make art more widely accessible. At Sonsbeek, however, within six years of its inception, the exhibition committee had built a pavilion, if only a temporary one. Why a pavilion, and why temporary? Because, as the English journal *Architectural Design* reported, the pavilion, 'provided spaces within which the sculptures were in scale, and textured backgrounds against which more fragile pieces, which would be lost in a natural setting, can be seen'.[4] There thus existed simultaneously the notion that sculpture could be seen better out of doors, and a realisation that this was not so.

The inherent instability of the premise of the sculpture park is manifested by the pavilion in that it exists at all, and then that it exists only temporarily. The pavilion in question was designed by Gerrit Rietveld, the veteran Dutch architect (then sixty-seven years old) who had recently triumphed with the Dutch Pavilion at Venice. This had been lauded as admirably fit for purpose, providing a simple white cube with cleverly diffused lighting. It was seen to suit Holland's self-image: plain but dignified, modest but self-aware. Whereas in Venice, Rietveld's pavilion marked national space alongside the plethora of other national pavilions, at Sonsbeek it was alone, in a park, and had the chance to become, if only temporarily, a special place in nature.

[3] Launched by the Institute of Contemporary Arts in London, with an exhibition at the Tate Gallery of the winning entries from a long international shortlist, this scheme was later understood to have been financed through the CIA. Another submission, by Wessel Couzijn, was also on show at Sonsbeek.

[4] 'Sculpture Pavilion, Arnhem, Holland', *Architectural Design*, December 1955, p.383.

7.1   Cover of *Forum*, no 4, May–June 1956

Rietveld's pavilion, which measured 12 by 12 metres, housed the vitrines that protected the smaller (large-ly historic) sculptures (7.1). In and around it were gath-ered the larger sculptures, presented on brick plinths. The space was varied but unified. A high central pavil-ion, open to the front, but protected by a canopy sup-ported on two columns, was bordered by two low pavilions and a covered walkway, each measuring 3 metres across. The canopy of the central pavilion was supported at its rear and sides by three cinder block walls with two areas of fenestration (7.2). The walls provided two kinds of backdrop: concrete breeze block and brick, and the blocks were used the 'wrong' way round, in different positions and with different bonds, to give different degrees of inten-sity (7.3). Sometimes a grid of circular holes might manifest itself across the walls, like large pencil marks on a sheet of cartridge paper. These might be set in

bands, so that a more open section would be bordered at top or bottom by greater infill, thus smoothing out the irregular patterning of the blocks. The walls were thus like screens which provided a low-key pattern and a sense of air and space.[5] The patterning made them seem less substantial, but also more discrete. The combination of 2-D and 3-D effects was to prove compellingly enduring.

This kind of plain but painterly—machine-made but hand-touched—background proved very sympathetic

[5] In his review of the pavilion when it was re-erected in Otterlo, J.P. Hodin admired the addition of coloured backgrounds—pale blue, pink and yellow—but found that the holes in the walls could be distracting. 'Le Pavillon Rietveld à Otterlo', *Quadrum*, XVIII, 1965, pp.154–5.

7.2   Gerrit Rietveld, Arnhem Pavilion, Sonsbeek Park, Arnhem, 1955

to sculpture. Its neutrality was sufficiently broken up
to provide some liveliness without distracting from
the sculptures themselves. The vast majority of these
were in bronze, and thus the palette was muted—
largely monochrome. Few sculptures on show were
over life-size and most were under. Portraits and
heads were shown at head height, under the covered walkway, which was itself almost domestic in
scale. The whole was modest, utilitarian, but strangely agreeable.

The ground was also given a hard surface, so that the whole pavilion was set against the grass and trees that surrounded it. The foliage was visible, but through glass, or beyond the paving. At Sonsbeek, we are in a park, not in the city centre. There is no sense of Scarpa's bridging of real space and museum space with solutions such as those he found for Cangrande, or even for the Canova plasters. A pavilion such as Rietveld's is built because without it the sculpture was insufficient. The sculpture would normally be in a museum (whence much of it had been obtained). The pavilion gives it a reason for being transported to a park, but it is doubtful whether it makes the sculpture look any better or more interesting than it would in the museum. It simply makes it more 'available'. In this case, the pavilion almost outstrips its brief, in suggesting itself at least as interesting as the artwork inside, if not more so.

Rietveld's Arnhem Pavilion was demolished after *Sonsbeek '55* and the materials were taken back into stock by the contractor, as intended by the architect[6] In 1958, on the occasion of Rietveld's seventieth birthday, the magazine *Forum* published a number of homages from architects including Le Corbusier, Richard Neutra and Alison and Peter Smithson. The young architect Aldo van Eyck (who was then forty) contributed a longer article called 'The ball bounces back'.[7] This was both a homage to Rietveld and an opportunity to voice contemporary concern, for Rietveld represented for Van Eyck the De Stijl heritage that had been lost or perverted by the generation which followed.[8] On Rietveld's seventy-fifth birthday, in 1963, a group of architects offered him the opportunity to have his pavilion rebuilt at the Rijksmuseum Kröller-Müller in Otterlo.[9] The critic J.P. Hodin contrasted its new siting with that at Sonsbeek, seeing it as much more open to the landscape at Otterlo, and thus more successful.[10]

The reconstructed pavilion, on a site selected by Rietveld, and now in a museum context, opened on 8 May 1965 with an exhibition of work by Barbara Hepworth. It was now recognised as being as much an artwork as the artwork it contained (7.4). This installation seems to have worked extremely successfully, with the holes in her sculptures echoing those of the pavilion, but with their richer materials setting them apart from its dusty matt walls.

[6] A. and P. Smithson provide this information in their homage to Rietveld, *Forum*, no. 3, March 1958, p.73.

[7] 'De bal kaatst terug', *Forum*, no.3, March 1958, pp.104–11.

[8] De Stijl had been at once historicised and re-discovered, most notably by means of the 1951 exhibition at the Stedelijk Museum in Amsterdam (an exhibition that Rietveld designed), and this late period was thus one of Rietveld's most productive. Two other possibilities for the pavilion's reconstruction had also been entertained; one for Vlaardingen and the other for Bergeyk. See M. Kueper and I. Van Zijl, *Gerrit Th. Rietveld: the complete works*, Utrecht, 1992, p.266.

[9] Anon., *statemuseum kroller muller otterlo,* a museum publication, 1969, pp.7, 50.

[10] J.P. Hodin, 'Le Pavillon Rietveld à Otterlo', *Quadrum,* XVIII, 1965, pp.154–5. Hodin was not completely convinced by the pavilion: though he compared it to the pleasure pavilions and *chinoiseries* of the eighteenth century, he saw it as insufficiently refined in its dimensions.

[11] Aldo van Eyck in *Aldo van Eyck, Works* compiled by Vincent Ligtelijn, Bussum, 1999, p. 134.

7.4   Gerrit Rietveld, Arnhem Pavilion (reconstruction), Rijksmuseum Kröller-Müller, Otterlo, 1965, showing Barbara Hepworth's *Squares with Two Circles,* 1963 in the foreground

It was a beautiful thing in an uncontroversial way and widely appreciated for it; a fairy tale that cannot be retold—though it was rebuilt on another site as a tribute to the architect.[11]

It was, moreover, now a memorial to Rietveld, who had died in 1964. In the same year as the pavilion was reconstructed at the Kröller-Müller, Van Eyck, who wrote this description, built a pavilion for Sonsbeek on exactly the same spot as Rietveld had done ten years earlier. It opened only a few weeks later. As is clear, Van Eyck admired the 'equipoise' of Rietveld's pavilion, which achieved an accord, in his view, between park, pavilion and people. Nevertheless, he wanted to do something different with his commission, partly because he questioned the reasons for showing art out of doors—'as though art has more to say (or says it more gently) when mother nature is there'—and partly because of the autonomy he noted in the art of the time. He saw in it a more urban character, which could be interpreted psychologically, using Van Eyck's words, as 'perplexing and provocative', 'kaleidoscopic and labyrithine'.[12] He therefore sought something of this clash in his design, and demanded that the viewer be close to the pavilion, or inside it, before he or she understood what happened inside.

The plans and models[13] that Van Eyck has left us not only show the labyrinthine or maze-like quality of this pavilion, but also mark out the positions of the various artists (7.5). Some of these artists are figurative (Marini, Wouters, César, Giacometti, González, Richier, Hajdu, Ipoustéguy), but more (Arp, Brancusi, Belling, Noguchi, Hepworth, Paolozzi, Pomodoro, Pevsner, Turnbull) are abstract or a surrealist mix of the two (Matta, Ernst). The works on show were strange creatures, and surrealism pervaded the space. Though most were in metal, the finishes were different, from dark green to polished brass. They were textured, unlikely and uncomfortable things, and the pavilion itself seemed eminently rational in comparison.

This was again built in concrete blocks, plain and unpainted. Six straight walls—creating five corridors —bulge out at different points to become semi-circular. Some of the 'apses' are one unit across, others two or three. The apses do not so much display the sculptures as allow people to walk round them, and round each other.[14] Three small round seats are complemented by two larger circular plinths and by one almost enclosed circular shaft. The light was even, and was filtered through translucent nylon stretched over steel tubes (7.6). Variation was provided in the construction of the apses, in which a kind of weave pattern emerged from the rectilinear blocks as they were set upon each other to create a curve (7.7). The plinths were made of the same material as the walls, and the whole was again placed on a concrete platform on the grassy field. Viewed from a distance, the pavilion was very light in colour and in its radiance shone out against the high, dark canopy of foliage above. It was reminiscent of some kind of illuminated glade. Overall there were strong similarities with Rietveld's pavilion of a decade earlier—above all in the siting, texture and colourway—and once

[12] Drawn from 'Pavilion, Arnheim, a place for sculpture and people', by Aldo van Eyck, pp.59–60 of World Architecture 4, Place and Environment, London, 1967, ed. by John Donat for Studio Vista London.

[13] These also show the changes that the structure underwent during this process, beginning more like a trefoil and then a four-leaved clover before finding its key solution in the mixing of straight and curved lines. See F. Strauven, Aldo van Eyck: The Shape of Relativity, Amsterdam, 1998, pp.500–6.

[14] In this respect, they differ from the design for the Loosduinen Church in the Hague (1963–6, built 68–9), which uses the curved baffle-like walls to give space and privacy to the devotional sculpture, but may well have been influenced by its architecture.

7.5   Aldo van Eyck, drawing for Arnhem Pavilion, 1965

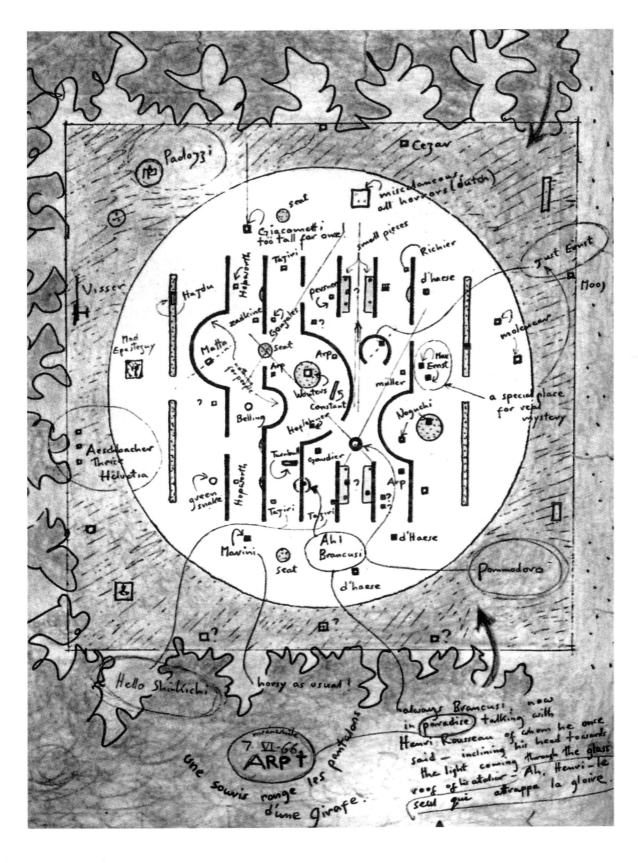

again there is a sense that the sculptures detract from the pavilion itself.

That the pavilion has become the artwork is amplified by a look at the wider context. Not only had other temporary exhibitions shown similar forms by other architects—most notably the Labyrinth for Children by BBPR at the 10th Milan Triennale in 1954 (7.8), which was reproduced in *Forum* in August 1959 next to one of Van Eyck's own playgrounds[15]—but artists had now begun to make permanent forms in which the sculpture created its own site, or the site the sculpture. Isamu Noguchi and Herbert Bayer had, by this date, demonstrated that 'sculptural sites' could just as successfully use earth or stones as sculpture, if not more so. Noguchi's UNESCO garden is much more cohesive than his sculpture gardens as such,

[15] *Il labirinto dei ragazzi* had a sculpture by Alexander Calder at its centre and a graffiti drawing by Saul Steinberg. See A. Piva, *BBPR a Milano,* Milan, 1982, p.99, fig. 54. See also Scarpa's 1952 Sculpture Garden for the Italian pavilion at the Venice Biennale, which uses a canopy of 'cut-out' circles to both protect the sculptures and provide light and shade. A. Albertini and S.Bagnoli, *Scarpa: Musei ed esposizioni,* Milan, 1992, fig.148.

7.6   Aldo van Eyck, Arnhem Pavilion, Sonsbeek Park, 1965

7.7   Aldo van Eyck, Arnhem Pavilion, Sonsbeek Park, 1965

in which his structures do not provide especially sympathetic homes to the sculptures of others.[16] His own forms do work, however, within his own spaces, and are interestingly interchangeable whether the spaces be commercial, ludic or commemorative. Noguchi's first designed spaces were playgrounds, and though it was many years before he was able to realise his designs, this interest in grouping forms within an enclosure has interesting connections with the post-war sculpture park. Van Eyck, however, was to design or supervise the construction or renovation of 735 playgrounds in Amsterdam over a period of thirty years from 1947.[17] Putting play into the heart of the city was his business, and the interior quality of the Sonsbeek pavilion was set up to be reminiscent of the city street.

In *The Situationist Times* of 1963, Van Eyck contributed a text entitled 'Labyrinthine Clarity'.[18] The journal itself was more like a book, and its topic was uniform: the labyrinth. Thus Van Eyck's contribution is one of many, and the pictures—of mazes, labyrinths, circular rock drawings and town-plans—follow a continuous sequence, from the beginning to the end of the volume. Among the other authors were Bachelard, Joyce and Kafka. Van Eyck's text is set somewhat like a Futurist manifesto, with varying point sizes, capitalisation and different indentations. In it he sets aside 'space and time' for 'place and occasion', which he sees as more important.[19] His aphorism 'labyrinthine clarity' is intended to encompass the ways in which place and occasion intersect: as both remembered and anticipated, consecutive and simultaneous.

Having established the need for an emphasis on place and occasion, Van Eyck suggests ways of creating it that focus on the relationship between big and small, and their transposition: 'a house is a tiny city, a city a huge house'. The next lines seem to presage exactly what Van Eyck was to build for Sonsbeek:

> Man still breathes both in and out, when is architecture going to do the same?

> When it does, watch the thin lines—those narrow borderlines—loop into the places people need; watch how they are persuaded to loop generously into a tiny-huge

[16] Bayer's *Marble Garden* and *Grass Mound* at Aspen both date from 1955, and pre-figure Robert Morris' 1966 *Project in Earth and Sod*. Noguchi's earliest designs for large-scale monumental works date to the 1930s, but were unrealised. Van Eyck had a lot more luck as a playground designer than Noguchi, who saw his designs rejected in New York for over thirty years. His first garden, in Tokyo, dates to 1952, and the UNESCO garden, his first significant work in this genre, dates to 1956–8. From then on, and especially after the sunken Beinecke garden at Yale (1960–4), Noguchi did a number of other commercial plazas. In 1965, his first sculpture garden opened at the Israel Museum, and his first playground was realised near Tokyo. It was Noguchi who was eventually to realise the Cullen Sculpture Garden at Houston (1977–86), with which Mies had earlier been involved.

[17] Van Eyck's admiration for the work of Sophie Taueber and Hans Arp is perhaps most obvious here.

[18] 'Labyrinthine Clarity', pp.79–85 of *The Situationist Times*, No. 4, October 1963, published in Paris and printed in Copenhagen.

[19] Colin St. John Wilson noted something similar in Rietveld's work: 'a spontaneous improvisation to serve the occasions of life, not a monument to conserve values'. *Architectural Review*, 136, 1964, p.402.

[20] Op. cit. (note 20), p.79.

[21] Giedion had singled out van Eyck's playgrounds at CIAM 1951 for admiration. The Sonsbeek pavilion might be seen to echo some of the Smithsons' interest in the street.

[22] An exception is his Nieuwmarkt playground of 1968, with its curvaceous wooden palisades, which is strangely reminiscent of the first MoMA sculpture garden.

[23] See Donat, above, p. 59.

7.8   BBPR, Labyrinth for Children, X Milan Triennale, 1954

INBETWEEN REALM
It is with thise [sic] in mind that I venture to call architecture
Built homecomming [sic].[20]

In its curvaceous apses, Van Eyck's Sonsbeek Pavilion seems to manifest and to enable the 'breathing out' and the 'breathing in' he describes, offering as it does the street punctuated by the lay-by. And in these apses, the visitors seek their homecoming. This works in a way that is reminiscent of but different from the playgrounds that Van Eyck had designed.[21] Those playgrounds had, from their outset, incorporated circular elements into their ground plans, but rarely did they have screens or walls, as at Sonsbeek.[22] High screens are not necessarily appropriate to children, who can be better supervised when playing in a more open space, but it is clear that this secretive maze-like quality was a key part of this project, and that the architect saw it as alluring. What is uncertain, however, is whether the screening did anything for the sculptures, or for the visitors' enjoyment of them. Van Eyck had cleverly noted that sculpture does not necessarily need the 'special grace' of 'mother nature',[23] but did he provide something more appropriate?

Though the pavilion may have been charming, the sculpture added little to its meaning. It was built for sculptures, but it would work without them. The sculptures would be as well off in a permanent gallery, while they did not fundamentally change the pavilion. They had no meaning in relation to it, and no function, either physical or narrative. Whereas Kolbe gave Mies' pavilion a special focus of concentration, and Fontana's Victory group summed up and transported the meaning of Persico's Salone, and Milles' sculptures were the object and the subject of Saarinen's Museum, fixed in place for decades, these sculptures were clearly temporary. If the function of sculpture is to be different, and special—to synthesise and concentrate human experience—then Van Eyck's pavilion did this as well, or better, than the sculptures it housed. His pavilion had no ceremonial or symbolic purpose—it was built simply to provide temporary shelter—but it went further than this, offering more pertinent comment about human behaviour than the art on show inside.

The sculptures themselves occupy the uneasy mid-1960s moment when sculpture does not know if it is figurative or abstract, and whether it is there to join up with architecture, or to stay apart from it. Though the works varied according to their approach to realism, they occupy a surprisingly similar form, which is to say, they are mostly of human height and monolithic; more or less replete (Hepworth) or eroded (Giacometti), assertive (Rik Wouters) or depressive (Isaac Witkin). They are on plinths. They seem like ornaments for Van Eyck's pavilion, which, in its greater spatial play and spectator interaction, in fact undermines their space. The works may have added a note of disquietude, like objects waiting for something to happen, but they seem displaced. Either Van Eyck has lost faith in sculpture, or his architecture betrays the fact that sculpture has lost faith in itself.[24]

Van Eyck knew about sculpture, almost from the inside. His friendship with the great critic Carola Giedion-Welcker, whom he got to know in Zurich during the war, and who had done so much not simply to promote modern sculpture, but to define it by placing it next to older forms (in nature and in culture), must have been highly influential. It is apparent in his own particular fondness for her own intimates, Arp, Sophie Taeuber and Klee. After the liberation of France, in 1944, Giedion-Welcker sent Van Eyck to Paris with provisions for Brancusi, and so Brancusi (and Joyce) entered his personal pantheon, as they had that of Giedion-Welcker.[25]

Giedion-Welcker also provided the link with the CIAM

[24] The exception, at this juncture, would seem to be Moore, and the critic for the *Museumjournaal*, A. Schulze Vellingausen, seems to feel obliged to admit this, despite himself: 'The most striking artist, in spite of some examples of megalomania, is Henry Moore, whose work is wonderfully displayed.' 1966, no.5 p.141. Moore, however, was largely displayed at some distance from the pavilion, in the park, where his large pieces, and those by Turnbull, Paolozzi and others, such as Mary Vieira and Shinkichi Tajiri, held their own against the foliage.

[25] 'A Tribute to Carola Giedion-Welcker', by Aldo van Eyck, *Forum*, 9, Nov. 1959, pp.321–2.

[26] The 'Bridgwater Questionnaire', compiled by Giedion, Arp and the English MARS group, was sent to each delegation in preparation for the 6th CIAM Congress in Bridgwater. Rietveld was asked to supply the Dutch reply; Van Eyck made his own independent response. The text can be found in Giedion's *CIAM A Decade of New Architecture*, Zurich, 1951, pp.30–9.

[27] In a 1939 essay, Rietveld had stated his view that 'the three plastic arts must develop completely independently of each other', and in 1959 he elaborated on this by explaining that as the present stylistic period was in its early phases, they should remain independent. M. Kueper and I. van Zijl, *Gerrit Th. Rietveld*, Utrecht, 1992, pp.50, 54.

[28] Just before the Smithsons went to Dubrovnik, they had been planning their exhibit at *This Is Tomorrow*, the exhibition which opened at the Whitechapel Gallery in August 1956. It was called 'Patio and Pavilion'. One might note that this exhibition began as a discussion about the 'belief that the arts should be able to again collaborate as in the Renaissance'. A. and P. Smithson, 'The "As Found" and the "Found"', in D. Robbins, *The Independent Group: Postwar Britain and the Aesthetics of Plenty*, Cambridge, Mass, 1990, p.201.

[29] 'The Team 10 Primer', edited by Alison Smithson and originally published in the English journal *Architectural Design* in December 1962, both starred and marginalised Van Eyck, using his poetic texts to open and close but not within the primer as such.

30 This is a paraphrase of the September issue of *Forum* (1959), which laid out 'het verhaal van een andere gedachte' ('the story of another idea') and is taken from the account given by Francis Strauven in his biography of Van Eyck, op. cit., pp. 339 ff. This issue of *Forum* was given to the participants at Otterlo 'previous to the start of the actual congress'. O. Newman, *CIAM '59 in Otterlo*, Stuttgart, 1961, p. 7.

group in which her husband Sigfried Giedion played such a central role. In 1947, Rietveld and Van Eyck both replied to Giedion's questionnaire on 'The impact of contemporary conditions upon architectural expression'.[26] While both agreed that each form—painting, sculpture and architecture—was autonomous,[27] Van Eyck believed that each must rediscover itself, and would only be able to cooperate with others when it knew what it was about itself. Echoing the Giedions' view, Van Eyck would stress the importance of both the imaginative and the political position in any discussion of architecture. The focus of the 1951 CIAM Congress, held in Hoddesdon, England, clarifies Giedion's continued importance for Van Eyck as a representative who understood the importance of, and the search for, the kind of meaning that might be better expressed by artists than by architects. The 1953, Aix Congress, with the participation of the Smithsons, brought home most clearly the new emphasis on society and its primordial patterns of living, and it was at Aix that the Smithsons, with Van Eyck, joined the team of younger architects that was given the brief to prepare for the 10th Congress in Dubrovnik in 1956.[28]

CIAM was founded on agreement and on diasagreement, and the 10th Congress, for which Team 10 had been set up, clarified for Van Eyck the areas in which he differed from the broader consensus. The convergences of interest between him and the Smithsons veil equally important differences, which emerged at Dubrovnik.[29] Van Eyck's own interest in the 'inbetween', in time, and in mass-production were excluded from CIAM but came increasingly to occupy him and his Dutch colleagues. In 1959, the Congress was held in Otterlo, at the Kröller-Müller Museum, and here all the members of Team 10 resigned. With this Congress, CIAM, which had first met in 1928, was definitively over.

Van Eyck's critique of CIAM was that 'another idea' —a built environment which reflected man and his different identities—had been neglected[30] In his view, CIAM's focus on problem-solving had led it to neglect the kind of new cultural vision that had been better expressed by painters, sculptors, poets, composers and scientists. Van Eyck's extensive interests in literature, science and anthropology meant that he drew on a wider range of sources than was customary. His close association with Cobra[31] (since 1947) gave him first-hand experience of working with artists, and he had, for instance, designed their first two exhibitions in 1949 and 1951, with shallow sloping bases, put together out of unusual materials, such as anthracite[32] The plinths echoed the paintings in their scale, almost suggesting that they had been laid out horizontally, but also constituted a kind of grid against which the paintings, in their gestural figuration, successfully played.

While the fine arts were part of Van Eyck's culture, he had a nuanced interpretation of what any *synthèse des arts* might mean. Moreover, his own work was increasingly encroaching upon the terrain of the 'fine artist'. Whereas the Cobra shows were simply installations within the classic galleries of the Stedelijk Museum and the Palais des Beaux-Arts in Amsterdam and Liège, the pavilion was all-encompassing. In a 1959 issue of the Dutch journal *Forum*, dedicated to the 'Nieuw Beelden league'[33] and the 'quest for mutual unity between the arts', with its wish to 'attain an integration of the hitherto isolated forms of art such as sculpture, painting, architecture, ballet, poetry etc', Van Eyck writes:

> Cooperation is possible and perhaps desirable./ Synthesis and integration are certainly not desirable. / Integration means impotence.[34]

Although it marked the end of an era, the Otterlo CIAM Congress was noted for the liveliness of its contributions, and Van Eyck's in particular. His chosen illustrations were of statuettes—from ancient civilisations —both to represent the continuity of human need, and to illustrate basic human relationships as they change from the single to the plural. This sense of continuity—illustrated by means of sculpted forms —surely comes out of Van Eyck's formation with Giedion-Welcker, who had used illustrations of neolithic circles alongside those of Brancusi in her own book, but it also throws light on his pavilion for sculpture, which was to be erected a few years later.

Van Eyck's concern with the 'in-between'—the threshold—went on being developed in the magazine *Forum*, which he continued to edit until 1963, and becomes clearly visible in the Sonsbeek Pavilion.[35] Its spiral or labyrinthine quality can be seen to repre-

[31] Van Eyck met Constant in 1947, who then introduced him to Appel and Corneille. In 1948, these and other artists formed the Dutch Experimental Group. *Cobra* (which stands for Copenhagen, Brussels and Amsterdam) appeared as a magazine from 1949.

[32] Anthracite was suited to Liège, a coal town, where the exhibition was staged, and contradicted the grandeur of the Palais des Beaux-Arts in a manner more appropriate to the *Exposition Internationale d'Art Experimental*, 1951.

[33] The 'Nieuwe Beelden' was founded in 1954 and principally set about its aims by means of creating and visiting exhibitions.

[34] *Forum*, no. 6, 1959, English summary at front.

[35] In these years he was also engaged on his written project 'The Child, The City and the Artist' (unpublished), for which he received a Rockefeller Foundation grant 1961–2. Strauven, op. cit., p.407.

sent his belief that history is cyclical rather than linear, and its form may well also represent his evolving interest in the inescapable relationship between the observer and the observed, as proven in recent scientific experiments, but revealed in art a long time since. This understanding of the interconnection of space and time, object and subject, interior and exterior, is deeply bound up with both Carola Welcker and Sigfried Giedion and with their writings. It was also very much part of a mid-century sculptural understanding, evident in sculptors whose work informed the Giedions, such as Arp and Hepworth. It is central to the interplay between sculpture and architecture, and would put pay to the kind of dualities this book has examined. In his understanding of what fine artists had to offer architects, Van Eyck went as far as, or beyond, the very artists who were his friends.

The relationship between the observer and the observed was made more clearly part of the subject by Van Eyck, whose pavilion proposed itself as the object and the subject. The nexus of viewer/viewed has long since become a subject for artists, many of whom have used an architectural vocabulary to speak to us about our own relationship with what we see and how we see it. 'Sculpture', as figurative or even as an abstract form, was no longer an additional feature. At one and the same time the viewer becomes the sculpture, as does the architecture.

CONCLUSION

1 Peter Smithson made this statement in a written reply to a BBC question in July 1956. It is quoted in *Places*, 7:3, 1991, in the first of four essays, 'Patio and Pavilion, 1956, reconstructed U.S.A. 1990', p.13.

2 A. and P. Smithson, Idem., p.14.

3 In a text of 1990, Alison Smithson described this exhibit as a 'pavilion in a patio', whereas the House of the Future (Ideal Homes Exhibition 1956) was 'a patio encapsuled by its pavilion'. Idem., p.10.

4 *This is Tomorrow*, Whitechapel Gallery, London, 1956, n.p.

The contribution by architects Alison and Peter Smithson to the 1956 London exhibition *This Is Tomorrow* consisted of a structure in which the artists Nigel Henderson and Eduardo Paolozzi laid out their work. Most of Paolozzi's sculptures (which were reminiscent either of archaeological finds or of children's clay impressions) were laid flat on the ground, rather than standing up. A few were placed on a simple low table. Henderson's collaged *Head of a Man* echoed the clay impressions in its texture, but also reminds us of earlier exhibition installations, from the 1920s and 1930s, in which dense amounts of photographic material, often with natural or industrial subjects, seen either very close-up or very far-off, were positioned within an architectural framework and served to convey the 'subject' of the presentation. Peter Smithson rationalised any 'inconsistencies' in the project in terms of his and his wife's role as architects, which was to provide the 'context for the individual to realise himself in'. It had fallen to the artists to give the 'signs and images to the stages of realisation'[1].

Two key points about this exhibit can be drawn out of a much later essay by the Smithsons: firstly, that it can be seen to be part of the argument about the synthesis of the arts (or 'collaboration'), and secondly that it was designed to 'include every visitor as an inhabitant'. Thus we might view this pavilion, like that of Van Eyck ten years later, as being about place and occasion, but, more importantly, as being about 'inhabitation'[2]. If Van Eyck's pavilion invited viewers in—asking them to engage with the building, and with the art inside—it also hinted at a change already in the air. It was the viewer who inhabited the space more actively than the art, which somehow seemed extraneous. This cue—that the figure in the pavilion need not be sculpted, but could simply be that of the viewer—is taken up and developed in the kind of work that effectively ends the period under review.

The title of the Smithsons' contribution was 'Patio and Pavilion'[3]. In the catalogue, they explained that the Patio represented the 'first necessity—a piece of the world', and the Pavilion, the 'second necessity—an enclosed space'[4]. Their exhibit makes real links with the pavilion as we have been discussing it, in terms of its providing shelter and a place for art. The links go further, for the roof was translucent and the interior was lined in reflective aluminium. Any visitor

Conclusion

5 A. and P. Smithson, 'The "As Found" and the "Found"', in D. Robbins (ed.), *The Independent Group: Postwar Britain and the Aesthetics of Plenty*, Cambridge, Mass, 1990, p.201.

6 Its ruined quality—it was later described by Reyner Banham and by Kenneth Frampton as something that might have survived a nuclear war—might again be compared to Johnson's Glass House, the central fireplace of which derived from the remembered image of a burnt-out village.

8.1   Alison and Peter Smithson, Nigel Henderson and Eduardo Paolozzi, 'Patio and Pavilion', *This is Tomorrow* exhibition, Whitechapel Art Gallery, London, 1956

to the 'pavilion' was thus immediately mirrored in its walls. But the whole had a roughly constructed homemade air: the 'pavilion' was more like a garden hut (the Smithsons later called it a *gîte*),[5] the patio more like a children's sandpit. This was almost a pastiche of the modernist pavilion, with its play on transparencies, on interiors and exteriors, and on the role of art (8.1).[6]

As sculpture takes on the vocabulary and scale of architecture, so architecture turns increasingly to the vocabulary of sculpture. As architects adopted an increasingly curvaceous (organic) vocabulary (which has often been described as sculptural), sculptors adopted the rectilinear structures more traditionally associated with architecture. I am thinking here of late work by Frank Lloyd Wright (the Guggenheim, completed 1959), Le Corbusier (Ronchamp, 1955), Alvar Aalto (Vouksenniska, 1956–8), of Oscar Niemeyer's work more generally, of Eero Saarinen (Idlewild Terminal, 1962), Jørn Utzon (Sydney Opera House, 1957), Pier Luigi Nervi et al. Alongside this, I am positing, most obviously, the work of American Minimalist artists such as Donald Judd, Robert Morris, Richard Serra and Carl Andre, who began showing in the mid-1960s.

The convergence of sculpture and architecture, and the increasingly important role of the viewer within the artwork, is demonstrated nowhere better than in Dan Graham's pavilions. Graham (b. 1942) had from the outset of his career in the late 1960s been experimenting with the components of the language with which art defines itself. Having worked first with the medium of the art magazine, he then became increasingly interested in the question of time, as manifested most clearly in new musical work by, for example, Steve Reich and Terry Riley. The way in which sonic repetition provided immediate feedback—in contrast to the delayed narrative of traditional melody—was something that he began to replicate and develop by means of cameras, monitors and mirrors. Such works, until then installed within a variety of existing interior spaces, took, from the mid-1970s, the logical next step of embracing the field of architecture.

Graham knew that Minimal art of the previous decade had referred to 'the gallery's interior cube as the ultimate contextual frame of reference'. As he wrote:

This reference was only compositional; in place of a compositional reading interior to the work, the gallery would compose the art's formal structure in relation to the gallery's interior architectural structure. That the work was equated to the architectural container tended to literalize it; both the architectural container and the work contained within it were meant to be seen as non-illusionistic, neutral and objectively factual —that is, as simply material. The gallery functioned literally as part of the art.[7]

From the late 1970s, Graham fuses container and contained. He does so in the form of the pavilion. His writings show how acutely aware he was of a specific twentieth-century lineage, which begins, like this book, with Mies van der Rohe. In his 1978 text 'Notes on *Public Space/Two Audiences*' (an artwork shown inside the Italian pavilion at the Venice Biennale of 1976), he explicitly states: 'I wanted it to function doubly as art and as simply an exhibition pavilion (for itself), following the examples of Mies van der Rohe's Barcelona Pavilion or Lissitzky's two exhibition rooms.'[8]

Graham differentiates his own work from Minimal art as well as from environmental/perceptual art.[9] His works are about the formal content of recent art, but they are also about experience, and in particular about the kind of 'just past' that he had first encountered in music, and then developed in film and video. His interest in new theories of viewing centred on the importance of the body, and of overlapping timeframes. He talks about being 'inside time', and his work explicates what happens inside the Barcelona pavilion itself. The experience of the Kolbe sculpture in the Barcelona Pavilion, which, I have argued, replicates the viewer's experience of the architecture, is now effected by the spectators themselves, within Graham's mirrored spaces. He does not need a sculpture in his pavilion, and nor does he need an architect to enclose it. The pavilion has become the sculpture. Whereas in Barcelona we return to the sculpture for a reprise of our own journey around the architectural interior, Graham's pavilions explicitly offer us up ourselves, again and again.

In a text from the same year,[10] Graham continues the Miesian story: 'In Mies' 1940s Farnsworth House,

[7] Dan Graham, 'My Works for Magazine Pages. "A History of Conceptual Art", 1965–69' (written in 1985), Dan Graham, Fundació Antoní Tapies, Barcelona, 1988, pp.61–2.

[8] *Two-way mirror power: selected writings by Dan Graham*, ed. A. Alberro, Cambridge, Mass., 1999, p.155.

[9] He cites Robert Irwin and Maria Nordman as examples of the latter practice.

[10] But first published in the Chicago Renaissance Society catalogue of 1981.

[11] 'Alteration to a Suburban House', (written 1978), idem., p.161, with extensive quotations also from Jeff Wall. See also note 4 in Graham's text on *Two Adjacent Pavilions* in his Tapies Foundation catalogue, 1998, p.133.

[12] Ibid. p.164. See also, for a slight variant, note 2 for the same text as above, p.132.

[13] The original setting of Graham's *Two Adjacent Pavilions*, at *Documenta 7*, with its choice of level or steeply descending approaches, was reminiscent of Johnson's pavilion at New Canaan, and both of them made reference to the traditionally uncertain scale of the distant folly. This work is also now at the Kröller-Müller Museum.

[14] Christian Norberg-Schulz, 'Talks with Mies van der Rohe', *l'architecture d'aujourd'hui*, September 1958, p.100. A slightly different version is given in Wolf Tegethoff, *Mies van der Rohe: Villas and Country Houses*, Cambridge Mass/New York, 1985, p.131, note 1.

[15] Dan Graham, 'Alteration to a Suburban House', 1978, from the Tapies Foundation catalogue, op. cit. at note 7, p.123.

the vertical glass curtain wall skyscraper pioneered by Mies in urban Chicago becomes a horizontal glass belvedere.'[11] At this time Graham began to make the pavilions which have since become synonymous with his practice as an artist.

In a third text from the same period, relating to his *Pavilion/Sculpture for Argonne*, he makes reference to another architect from this story: 'Because of its double function as architectural pavilion and as a sculptural form, a comparison could be made to Rietveld's sculpture pavilion ... which is both a sculptural and a utilitarian form.'[12] As Graham notes, the confusion does not lie simply in the fact that architecture has become sculpture. It lies also in the fact that the pavilion is in nature. Set in nature, it achieves isolation and independence, but its role is nevertheless ambiguous.[13] The close alliance with nature confuses us: is this structure a shelter or a work? And do we look out from it, or at it? Is nature part of its subject? Is it a belvedere which captures the view, or is it a pavilion which captures the art?

In an oft-repeated answer from a 1958 interview, Mies had declared:

> Nature should also live its own life, we should not destroy it with the colors of our houses and interiors. But we should try to bring nature, houses, and human beings together in a higher unity. When you see nature through the glass walls of the Farnsworth House it gets a deeper meaning than outside. More is asked for from nature, because it becomes part of a larger whole.[14]

Graham develops precisely this line of thinking in his description of what is happening in the glass houses of Mies and of Johnson:

> Nature is seen on all sides and, in the optical merger of its image with the reflections of the interior space on the glass curtain wall, interior and exterior are made identical. Instead of a dialectical opposition between nature, man-made architectural form, and life-style, the glass building combines these into a 'utopian' language of pure transcendental materiality.[15]

In 1965, Rietveld's 1955 pavilion was reconstructed at the Kröller-Müller Museum in Otterlo. In 1986 Mies'

1929 pavilion was reconstructed in Barcelona. In 2006 Van Eyck's 1966 Sonsbeek pavilion, like that of Rietveld, was also reconstructed in Otterlo.[16] Three temporary pavilions are made permanent; three pavilions that no longer have to 'do' anything. Does their change in temporal status affect their status as 'artworks'? Have they become artworks, or were they always artworks, function or no function?

The Sonsbeek pavilions work as well or better without artworks inside them. Graham's fascination with the pavilion as a form makes this clear, and shows how the alliance between modernist architecture and sculpture has changed. Sculpture is no longer used for its fundamental difference, as it was at Barcelona, where the figurative sculpture was very much part of the constructive plan.[17] As the disciplines have become more similar, they have become less complementary. The sculpture has become abstract, and architectural, and we the viewer, are the figure. We look at the pavilion, and out from the belvedere. We choose our view, and whether or not to be in it (8.2).

[16] Otterlo was, ironically enough, the scene of Van Eyck's historic resignation from CIAM.

[17] In a late interview with Katherine Kuh, Mies points out that he likes 'to come upon a fine work of art and then find a place for it'. The two disciplines exist apart at the beginning, and may be brought together only later. 'Mies van der Rohe: Modern Classicist', *Saturday Review*, 23 January 1965, p.61.

8.2 Dan Graham, *Two Adjacent Pavilions*, 1978–82, *Documenta*, Kassel, 1982